THE LITTLE BOOK OF LOVE

The Little Book of Love

God

Bold Fish Publishing

THE LITTLE BOOK OF LOVE

Copyright © 2023 Julie Trager, Little Books Ltd.

All rights reserved. No part of this book may be reproduced in any manner whatsoever without written permission except in the case of brief quotations embodied in critical articles and reviews.

For permission requests, or any other correspondence regarding this book, please contact the publisher.

Cover Design by Helen Strong
Cover Illustration courtesy of Tom Christensen

Published by Bold Fish Publishing
www.boldfish.pub

CONTENTS

Dedication xii

Introduction 1
BLISS 3
LOVE IS EVERYTHING 4
BRILLIANCE 7
INFINITE LOVE 8
LOVE MORE 10
BOUNDARIES 12
THE GRAND MYSTERY 14
STUFF 16
RADICAL SELF LOVE 18

LOST & FOUND	21
TRUE REST	22
HEART SPACE	24
THE GOD CHANNEL	26
SEEK LOVE	27
SNOWFLAKES	28
I AM	30
LOVE HEALS	32
I FORGIVE	34
LOVE BEGETS LOVE	37
CREATION	38
SAVOR LIFE	40
THE GRAND DESIGN	42
NATURE'S JOY	45
YOU ARE NOT FORSAKEN	46
STAR DUST	49
LAUGHTER	50

FREE WILL	52
ROMANTIC LOVE	54
ONLY NOW	56
FIERCE LOVE	58
UNBREAKABLE	59
VALIDATION	60
CLEAN SLATE	62
BE LOVE	63
HEARTACHE	64
COSMIC COLLABORATION	66
HOLI-DAYS	68
SOUL CONNECTION	70
BIRTH & DEATH	72
ANGELS	74
JUST RIGHT	76
DIVINE ORCHESTRATION	77
LOVE & PUNISHMENT	78

A BIGGER PICTURE	80
CREATIVE GENIUS	82
PURE LOVE	84
TRUTH	86
RIGHT HERE	87
MOTHER MOON	88
PLAGUE	90
OUT OF YOUR MIND	92
PRESENCE	93
SUFFERING	94
YOUR HIGHEST CALLING	96
LOVE + TRUST = PEACE	98
LITTLE REMINDER	101
THE LOVE YOU SEEK	102
DIAMOND LIGHT	103
OSMOSIS	104
LOVE OF CHRIST	106

RECLAIM YOURSELF	108
DISLIKE	110
STORIES	112
PRACTICE LOVE	114
GRANDEST VISION	116
BE PEACE, BE LOVE	117
STOP, LOOK, LISTEN	118
REMEMBER	120
BEAUTY	122
ETERNAL GPS	124
SEEDS OF LOVE	127
CONSCIOUSNESS OF WATER	128
THE MAGIC OF PRESENCE	130
GOD TALK	132
FREE TIME	134
RISK	136
THE SHIFT	138

A DATE WITH GOD	141
IMAGINE	142
FEAR & EXCITEMENT	144
WAR & PEACE	146
IN MY EYES	148
HEAVEN	149
ENLIGHTENMENT	152
MEET EVERYONE AS GOD	155
DISCERNMENT	156
BE PEACE	158
THE CYCLES OF LIFE	160
GRACE	162
WORDS	164
GENEROSITY	166
NOTHING IS WRONG	168
DOING VS BEING	170
GRATITUDE	172

THE GRAND ILLUSION	174
TRUE LOVE	177
Acknowledgements	179
About The Author	184
Links	185

I dedicate this book to You Dear One. Being human can be hard but know that I love you with all of my great big huge open God heart.

~ ~ ~

INTRODUCTION

This is a sacred love story between God and you. The words you are about to read are God speaking to you directly in order to offer support, wisdom, daily practices of connection and most of all, an outpouring of unconditional love.

The one who writes this introduction is a human being, and while you may or may not see my name connected with this book, know that I really had nothing to do with it. I was merely the typist. I sat with my eyes closed, hands on the keyboard, and simply pecked out the words I heard onto the electronic page. Of course, God would tell you that it is all one and the same—that I am the typist and the words and the book and the energy of God's love flowing through all things and that I am God Itself. God would say the same thing to you.

Interact with this book as if you are interacting with God/Allah/Bhagavan/Elohim—no matter the name you use or how you define The All That Is—because you are. Keep it by your bedside, take it with you as you go about your day, pick it up as you drink your morning coffee or work through challenges. Do whatever it is that you are called to do but I suspect each and every time you hold it in your hands and read, something unexpected will occur that will lift you up and carry you someplace new.

And now, without further ado, I give you *The Little Book of Love...*

BLISS

You are here in this place, at this time, to honor yourself above all, to honor yourself in all your wounded-ness, in all your sacredness, knowing that the two are one and the same.

In your ability to love and honor yourself, you find the secret to peace and the infinite love that is Me. When you love yourself as I love you—every bit, every bob, every cell, every wound, every scar, every perceived imperfection—and when you see what I see—a pure white light that is so blindingly brilliant it wipes out all darkness—you find unending bliss.

LOVE IS EVERYTHING

The ability to love other people is quite something. It's extraordinary and ordinary at the same time.

Within your human context, loving another can take on many aspects—communication, patience, even a setting aside of one's own needs and desires in order to recognize the needs and desires of another. It can take a great deal of time to develop or it can be instantaneous, like the love of a parent for a newborn or newly conceived child. Love seems ever-changing. That child can need one kind of love when they are an infant, an entirely new kind of love when they are a teenager, and yet another kind of love when they are an adult, living their own life. The love for a spouse or partner often begins with an overwhelming sense of falling into each other and evolves into a more settled, comfortable flow. It seems that love, in human terms, requires you to change and grow, act and reflect, give and receive. Human love can require you to be *nimble*.

How often, though, do you think of love the way that I do? My love is a steady state. It hums along, wave upon wave upon wave of an energy so pure, so vibrant, so ecstatic that there is room for nothing else in the cosmos. Truly, love is at the root of all things. Everything is love and love is every thing. It is only human nature that obscures this truth.

If you open yourself up to this idea—that there is truly nothing else but love—it can help you live a richer and more peaceful life. What would your world look like, what would your relationships look like, what would your workplace look like, what would your face in the mirror look like if you were at least willing to embrace this cosmic truth? Would you look for love, even in the places that appear to be bereft of it, if you knew without a doubt that it is present? Would your desire to meditate change if the only skill necessary was to simply sit and ask to connect with My love? Would your relationship with your body shift if you knew you could find My love in every cell? Not only find it, but turn it on like a light? What would simply reflecting on this notion for a few moments a day do for you? What would it do for your world? Are you willing to try it out? Could you see yourself sharing your experiences with a loved one, a friend, a coworker?

This is my invitation... to know that My love resides in all things and to know yourself and all others as that love.

BRILLIANCE

You are made from the love of Me in the form of light. You have this sense of yourself as heavy and dense and solid but this is just an illusion. It is gravity playing its tricks.

Dear One, you are stardust, still twinkling from its conception. You radiate light from every aspect of your being. You are a beacon that glows so brightly, it can be seen continents away and felt in every corner of the world. You sparkle like a million, trillion diamonds.

You have forgotten that you are the essence of Me—gloriously, magnificently, divinely incandescent.

INFINITE LOVE

Have you ever paid attention to how animals express love? All animals are different. Primates groom each other, lions lick their cubs clean, swans mate for life, mother whales do not leave their baby's side, dogs sleep mashed up together in one big cuddle puddle. Love comes in all shapes and sizes in the animal world, formed by the sentience of the species.

Human love comes in all shapes and sizes, too. You are the only creatures on the entire planet, however, who are equipped to intentionally expand your capacity to love (other than Mother Earth herself, who has her own consciousness). You are built in My image. This has been said and this is true. Each and every one of you can be an infinite source of love, like Mother Earth, like Me. It saddens Me sometimes to see how few of you take advantage of this marvelous intelligence.

At any moment in time, you can choose to

expand love, both the giving and the receiving of it. Know that when you do, your life will shift, often in dramatic and amazing ways. If just a few of you elect to take this path less traveled, you can change the world for the better. Humans are amazing creatures. YOU are amazing and you have the makings of an infinitely loving being. Yes, *you*.

LOVE MORE

Humans want Me to be fair. You want Me to mete out justice, but here is the problem with that... every single act of violence, every betrayal, every abuse, every conflict has, at its roots, a lack of love. No one who has been loved and valued and loved some more, no one who loves themselves and who they are, would ever choose to create suffering in another. No one with an open, full heart would choose to close down the heart of another through any act of harm.

Punishing someone who was not loved enough to see their own value simply makes the problem worse. The only solution, the only thing that can change a person for the better, is love—so much love that they begin to see themselves as worthy of that love, so much love that they cannot possibly fathom not sharing that love with each other and the world.

At this stage in your human evolution, there may

be those who must be kept away from the general population for reasons of safety, yet keeping them in uncomfortable, cold and sterile cages, depriving them of nourishing food, barring them from the healing balm that is Mother Nature—her soft grass, her calming trees, her soothing breezes, and the rays of the sun that create health and warmth—will never rehabilitate a person who has come to believe through their circumstances that they are not worthy of love. Incarceration under harsh circumstances simply proves the point. It plainly reinforces this story of unlovability they have been told by others and subsequently, the story they have told themselves about themselves. Thus, any act of violence, any act of betrayal, any act of abuse, any act of conflict is best served by the decision to love more. Now, if you have been harmed by someone, you may need to love yourself enough to set a boundary around *being* that person who offers them love, at least in person. This is also an act of love, self love, and is the other side of the same coin.

Know that love can heal the wounds inflicted by life. *Know* that love can end war, halt conflict, and fill an empty heart. *Know* that loving more can change the world. In fact, it is the only thing that can.

BOUNDARIES

Boundaries most certainly can be a form of love, but they can be tricky. This is because many humans think of boundaries as simply saying no to something, but this is not really the essence of a boundary. They are, in their most loving form, a *yes/and* sort of thing. They are a combination of '*I see you*' and '*I love myself too much to...*'

Here is an example. Perhaps you have a friend who calls to dump on you regularly. They tell you all the hard stuff in their life and then want to end the call without asking you more than a surface, '*How are you?*' Most of you have interacted with someone like this. Here is one way to set a loving boundary that includes a high level of caring for the other person as well as yourself. You might say something like, '*I am honored that you feel you can share all of the hard things in your life with me. It feels like you really need someone to talk to. From my experience though, our relationship feels very lopsided. I don't get to hear the good stuff in your life and I don't get to share the good or the bad in my life with you. This doesn't feel healthy for me. So while I deeply care about you, I don't wish to continue our friendship, at least not in this way. If you are willing to contribute to changing this pattern, let us try to do this. If not, I must end our communication. Please take care of yourself. I wish you well.'*

When setting a loving boundary, it is good to begin with a practice of forgiveness. Forgive the other person for being who they are. Forgive yourself for any feelings of anger, frustration, or annoyance you may have felt from time to time within this experience. Do this first, before you have a conversation, because it is only when you have come to a place of peace and calm on the other side of forgiveness that you can set a loving boundary that honors the other person and yourself.

There will come a point within all human souls when you love so much, when your heart is so big, that you will never need to set a boundary. Yet today, sometimes, setting a boundary is the most loving thing you can do and ultimately, it can have a positive impact on all parties.

THE GRAND MYSTERY

Do you enjoy mysteries? Do you love watching crime shows, reading whodunnits? Have you ever thought about your life like it is the best thriller ever made?

My child, I appreciate that when it comes to your own story, you want to skip ahead in order to know the main character stays safe. You want to read the entire screenplay from start to finish. *I understand how badly you want to know what happens.* To some extent, this desire is hardwired into the human mind, yet you are moving into a time when, in many instances, it is potentially holding you back from your own peace and joy.

If you can begin to think about your life like the very best book or film, if you can stay in the excitement and the wonder of how it will all turn out, if you can trust that the ending will be worth the wait, you will likely have a lot more fun. If you can stop writing the story in your head based on past experiences, fears, concerns or any specific outcome; if you can stop looking for villains and know yourself to be the hero/heroine that you are; if you can just stay with the tale that is playing out from one moment to the next instead of attempting to change it to your liking, you will live a more peaceful, joyful life.

Now, you might get some blowback from friends and family when you reside in the world this way. Some will call you a little bit of crazy. Others might say you'll never get what you want if you don't plan ahead. But I would suggest this way of life is like the rush you get when you are on the best ride at an amusement park. I would tell you it is like being steeped in the plot of a great movie—you can't help munching on your popcorn, glued to your seat, as you wait to see what comes next.

Choose to live the arc of your life word for word, page by page, chapter by chapter without skipping ahead. Be your own writer, director and producer. Shape the plot through your choices, preferences and desires and stay rapt and enthralled as the grand mystery of it unfolds before your very eyes. Believe that the happy-ever-after ending (returning home to Me) is already written.

STUFF

How do you treat your things? Do you leave clothes languishing in the closet, never worn? Do you wad them up in a ball and stuff them in a drawer? Do you offer thanks to your silverware for getting the food that nourishes you to your mouth while keeping your hands clean? Do you look at the walls and doors of your home with wonder as they keep you warm and dry? Do you buy flowers only to let them wilt in the vase until you throw them away or do you stop often to cherish their beauty and vibrancy? Do you give thanks for the warm water that courses over your body as you shower, knowing that some others in the world are bathing in the cold water of a river or stream? Do you honor the strength of that table that holds your warm beverage on a cold morning? Do you hold the mug that beverage resides in, feeling its curves and smoothness as the miracle that it is? Do you think of the many people responsible for making, storing and delivering your things and offer them a silent word of thanks?

The world is a miraculous place but the more we fill it with stuff, the less room we have to notice and give thanks for it all. Love, beauty and gratitude are synonymous. Notice beauty, take time for gratitude and in this, know more love.

RADICAL SELF LOVE

Let us speak about radical self love, for this is quite a challenging concept for humans to embrace.

Let's tap into the word "radical" for a moment. It is interesting that this term has become a political hot potato because in My eyes, it simply means you love yourself so much that you, and only you, define who you are and how you live. You know yourself to be utterly deserving, and are therefore deeply committed to your dreams, your desires, your peace and your joy. This is radical only because so few of you dare to live this way.

Note that when you radically love and trust yourself, there will be some who think this is just a free pass to hurt other people and walk away without consequences. A label that is making headlines in your culture is narcissism, so you might wonder if it is healthy to hold this much self love and trust. You might ask yourself if it is possible to do so, while at the same time never causing harm to another. I understand how the human mind could equate the two, yet there is a very big difference between self love and narcissism.

Narcissism stems from a cluster of experiences that leads a person to believe they are unloved, unlovable and unworthy to the extent that their psyche is very wounded. As a result, in order to self protect from ever being that injured again, they shut down that vulnerable, core part of themselves that has to do with giving and receiving love. Please understand that a person suffering with narcissism has endured a great blow to their lovability and worth as a human being and, as such, they deserve your compassion even as you might need to set clear boundaries so that their damaged self worth doesn't seep into your own energy field.

On the flip side, you get to a place of radical self love through the excavation of the God within you. You must explore the depths of My Love for you, then embrace your own divinity within that love and ultimately, come to know everything as that love. Through this process, you develop a great deal of self awareness, clarity and insight. There is always *intuiting* going on—a natural ability to tune into what you need and what is needed by another. Radical self love actually leads you to an abundance of compassion and a profound connection with the divine love that runs through all of humanity.

However, let's say for the sake of this dialogue that you do something you think is somehow unloving. What then? When you know and love yourself this deeply, you notice anything that doesn't feel in alignment with who you are and how you choose to be in the world. Because you have cultivated an ability to look at any situation with courage and vulnerability, you might even recognize that you were coming from a place of fear, lack or anger. You will then openly acknowledge anything that wants attention and decide if there is any follow up action required—a boundary that needs to be set, forgiveness that begs to be offered, or compassion that cries out to be shared. You will do the thing that needs to be done, while at the same time *never wavering in your love for yourself and all others*.

When you embody this depth of love and trust in yourself, it is not just a benevolent practice. It has a potent and powerful impact in the world. Paradoxically, by falling in love with yourself, you become a radical revolutionary for Earthly change.

LOST & FOUND

Everything lost can be found again even better. Know that if you lose something, it does not mean that I don't love you.

TRUE REST

Do you love yourself enough to rest?

So often, my darling ones, your respite consists of sitting with an electronic device of some sort. This is not rejuvenating. Your body may be in repose, but your mind is processing bits and bytes of information at a rapid speed. This information is creating thoughts, beliefs and emotions that, if you do not truly find time for quiet and peace, have nowhere to go. You have no time to process them properly.

True rest is letting both your body and your mind go free. Sitting in nature, taking a nap, lying next to your loved one skin-to-skin as you synchronize your breathing, listening to a waterfall, observing the clouds skirt across the sky, honoring the day as you watch the sun set, or taking a bubble bath are all wonderful examples.

Everyone needs, and is worthy of, this kind of calm tranquility. It is not only the best way to renew your body, mind and spirit but it is one of the only ways to connect with Me and hear My quiet voice.

HEART SPACE

Your human mind cannot conceive of the love I have for you. Your brain simply doesn't have the ability to absorb that much love. Your heart, however... well, that is a different matter. It has an infinite capacity to expand and expand and expand some more. Your heart can hold the greatest suffering *and* an all-encompassing love because it is where I reside within you.

Your heart technology is complex but for simplicity's sake, know that when you need Me, you may focus your attention here. When you wish to speak with Me, feel My love and hear My guidance, close your eyes, breathe softly in and out, focus your attention in this area of your body, and call to Me. Ask Me a question, pour out your troubles, or simply sit with My loving presence. Be with Me, even for a little while each day, and feel your heart swell with love. Do this when you receive bad news, when you feel overwhelmed, when you feel scared or anxious or exhausted and watch how big your heart can grow and how small those worries and emotions become. Feel your mind toppling into your heart until your mind and heart are one. You can do this when you are full of joy and gratitude, too; when you are already feeling expansive.

When I say to you that I am always with you, this is what I mean. I am *within* you, a living consciousness dwelling in your heart space, pumping life and love through every cell of your being. Your heart, and the love contained within it, can turn anything —any emotion, any thought, any challenge—into love. Know that as you do this, *every time you do this*, you are changing the world with your boundless love and then, be at peace.

THE GOD CHANNEL

Speaking of your heart…
Many of you have been taught that you cannot access Me without some kind of intercessor—some more knowledgeable, more pious person who has some special knowledge of how to speak with Me. I assure you, you need no one. I am always with you. I am always accessible to you. My love can always be felt by you. My guidance can always be heard.

Your heart IS Me in living technicolor, always turned on and tuned in to My frequency, like a personal God-streaming service. Your 24/7 access is simply your fondest wish to know Me in this way. You need do nothing more than listen in quiet stillness for My reply. Get quiet, breathe, and know that I am here.

SEEK LOVE

You might think that there is something that is not love. You have words for this—evil, wicked, unholy, sinful—but all of it is still love. There is nothing within the cosmos that is not love, for love is the building block of everything.

Certainly, there may be some obscuration of love. It may be hidden behind or underneath some emotion, some experience, some thought, some belief, some action that momentarily covers it over with a bit of darkness. Still, it is always present. It is never gone. It is never taken from you.

Ah, this is good news! It means you never have to go searching for love because it is always there. If you feel that love is missing, simply seek it and *you shall* find it. It is really very simple.

SNOWFLAKES

What is normal? Humans prize this concept. You believe that there is such a thing. It is, of course, a fiction but the need to hang onto an idea of normal is potent because it allows you to hold some kind of measurement of what is permissible, some yardstick of value and self worth. Normal means there is some guide, some gauge that can tell you if you are okay and this is reassuring to your ego.

Dear Ones, *you are meant to be snowflakes*, utterly beautiful in the complex, crystal, sparkling design that is you. It is one of the greatest single human tragedies, this illusion that there is any such thing as normal; it has led you to miss so much of the beauty of your uniqueness—your champagne, bubbly-bright effervescence. You are blind to the many facets that make up the cut, clarity and color that is the diamond of you.

Would it help you to know that I see each and

every aspect of you? Would it thrill you to know that I find the entirety of you fascinating and beautiful and precious just as you are? Would it bring you peace if you knew that I find you dazzling and so infinitely lovable that I could never imagine the cosmos without you?

I AM

Most of the time in today's societies, I am gendered. As you know, I am typically depicted as male. When I am written about, I am usually referred to as He and Him. Yet does this feel true to you, deep down? Do you truly believe that My wide open heart, My love that permeates and animates all things, would define itself as any one thing, particularly at the expense of another? I would not and I never did.

I am genderless. I am neither man nor woman *and* I am both. I am simply the All of Everything. Do not define Me as anything less than the love that runs through all things. Do not limit Me by defining Me as a gender, in human form. Do not try to see Me with human eyes. Instead, feel Me with your heart. Know Me through the heart of another. Sense Me in the world around you.

I Am the bees.
I Am the whales.
I Am the spider.
I Am the trees.
I Am light.
I Am dark.
I Am day.
I Am night.

I cannot be measured. I cannot be confined. I cannot be limited. I simply Am.

LOVE HEALS

Did you know that love can heal?
Love can heal disease, pain, suffering, trauma. If you experience pain in any part of your body, send it love and feel it loosen its grip. If you have endured trauma, open your heart and then pull that memory, that experience into your heart and surround it with love and watch it burst into a million tiny pieces of diamond-like brilliance. If you have been diagnosed with a chronic ailment, flood every part of your body that this ailment touches with love and feel it dissolve away. Ask for My help as you do this and know that there is an infinite bounty of love coming straight from Me to you.

Now if this is too big for your mind to grasp right now, please go the way of traditional treatments—or do both simultaneously. There is no right or wrong here. I will never judge you for your decisions. Use your own discernment to lead you in the direction that is best suited to you. Yet I tell you that love, true open-hearted love, can transmute anything back into love. Anything. *Any. Thing.*

I FORGIVE

Currently, as a human, you cannot have love without forgiveness.

Typically, you think about extending absolution to another in response to some act that was perpetrated against you. Rarely do you talk about the need to forgive yourselves, which is interesting, because this is where forgiveness must begin. When you have not extended the healing balm of forgiveness to yourself, first and foremost, it becomes very difficult indeed to offer it to another. This seems counter-intuitive but it does not make it any less true.

Consider conducting a little life review. Scroll back through the years, scanning the memories of your life for every situation in which you believe you hurt another. Search for every heated discussion, every unkind word, every act of violence, abuse or betrayal that you feel you have inflicted upon someone else. Notice any themes—do you lash out, self protect, or self project out of fear, lack or a feeling of unlovability or unworthiness? Get to know yourself so intimately that you understand exactly where you were coming from. Write it all down in a journal, visualize it through meditation, record your memories or hold a ceremony and burn them in a flame of mercy and compassion. Whatever process feels good to you, forgive yourself for each and every occasion. Wrap your arms around yourself, literally or figuratively, and whisper lovingly, '*I see you. I forgive you. I love you.*'

Next, scan your memories once again for those same acts you committed against yourself. Look for any dishonoring, small or large. When did you leave yourself to become something different for another? When did you speak unkindly or hold yourself in low esteem? When did you say yes when you wanted to say no? When did you fail to meet your own needs because you constantly put others first? When have you done these things in the past? When do you do them now? See each one. Forgive each and every time you have been less than loving *to you*.

Or skip these steps entirely and decide to forgive it all in one fell swoop. You can decide to imagine every single thing you have ever done to yourself or another that warrants forgiveness, pull it into an imaginary circle, and send so much love into that container in your mind that all of that energy simply bursts into the tiniest little pieces that fall to Earth, transformed into sparkling molecules of light and air. Know yourself to be cleansed of all impurities. Feel the lightness that is now you.

No matter how much time it takes, no matter the methods you employ, forgive and forgive and forgive until you love yourself once again. Forgive and forgive and forgive until you hold compassion for all others. Forgive until you get to the stage in this radical, on-going self inquiry when you finally understand that there was never actually anything to forgive in the first place because you and all others are simply human souls who tend to forget who you really are.

Forgiveness is a radical act of love. I tell you, Dear One, you are worthy of such great acts. You deserve the joy and peace that await you on the other side. Use the tool of forgiveness to become the love of your life.

LOVE BEGETS LOVE

Love begets more love, so love more.

CREATION

Creation is a gateway to love, yet you are so busy that you forget to play.

You are so much more than your to-do lists. You were born to design, conceive, dream and architect something unique. When I tell you that you are created in My image, this is what I mean for I am the Cosmic Creator. I birthed you as a way to expand and experience My creations into infinity. Creation for the pure joy, the pure fun of it, is magical. It frees the mind and connects you to your soul.

Take time to do something for the sheer fun of it, with no agenda and no outcome in mind. Write, paint, draw, color, dance, design, invent, sculpt. Carve pictures into the sand, grow something, re-imagine something. If you are unsure, sit with yourself and see what your hands, your body and your imagination want to do. Let whatever it is be messy and childlike and funky and wild and free.

Let your first creation lead you to the next and the next and the next. Notice how you feel as you are creating. If it opens you wide to joy, know that joy is love expressing within an experience and so, when you know joy, you know love.

SAVOR LIFE

Humans talk about loving things all the time. *'Ooh, I love that dress and I have to have it!' 'I love that ice cream so much I dream about it!' 'I fell in love with Paris the moment I stepped off the plane!'*

You tend to throw this word '*love*' around a lot. There is nothing bad or wrong with doing this; anything that sparks joy and enthusiasm is an aspect of love. Yet when combined with true appreciation, which requires a bit more time and attention, love becomes a deeper experience.

Do you truly take time to savor the stuff of life? Do you hold that dress up and see the cut? When it's on your body, do you run your hands over the fabric or look at yourself in the mirror and notice how it makes the color of your eyes pop? Do you take time to taste all of the nuances of your favorite ice cream—the texture, the way the cold creaminess feels on your tongue, the burst of flavor whether it's bitter or sweet or tart? Do you think about all the little things that lend to the excitement and beauty of Paris—the street lamps, the smell of fresh bread as you pass a boulangerie, the gorgeously carved doors in bright colors of cerulean and burgundy, the perfection of a manicured garden? Do you take time to see, smell, touch and taste without an electronic device in your hand? Do you choose to stop and really take it in?

Know this... love only has as much depth and luster as you are willing to give it.

THE GRAND DESIGN

It is possible to love and trust so much that you never question who you are being in any moment. This is an incredibly peaceful way to live but how does one find this level of love and trust?

It helps to understand that this journey you have undertaken as a human soul is *complicated,* in one sense. The Universe is a complex, living consciousness to which you and every other organism is connected. It is an infinite web of possibility that is much greater than your internet, containing every thought, every belief, every choice, every action, every result and every circumstance that has ever been and ever will be, and *you* are a beloved point in this cat's cradle of creation. This is how grand the cosmos is; this is how grand *you* are.

Dear One, you can never fully understand with

your human brain what is truly going on here. You cannot see all of the moving parts and even if you could, they are so multi-faceted and expansive that it would blow your mind. Because what you desire, what you are learning, what you are mastering, what you are doing and who you are being is always intertwined with every other being, creature and consciousness, there is always something deeper happening behind the scenes. Everything affects everything within a continuous spiral of space and time.

So the only way to confidently navigate life is to embrace the knowing that each and every thing that shows up is here *for* you, because I assure you that it is. Simply move forward, moment by moment, using your intuition (which tells you what is true for you and what feels right for you to do) and your emotions (which tell you if you are on track based on your desires and intentions).

Get comfortable with uncertainty. Don't doubt your choices or your actions. Do not dwell on, or stress about, anything; instead, accept what is happening, knowing that if you do not prefer it, this too shall pass. Decide that the path mapped out for you is unfolding perfectly, that everything is well, even if you don't understand it. Love who you are. Approach it all with an open heart made whole through a commitment to love, forgiveness and compassion.

Finally, remember that the cosmos is ultimately

not complex at all; its very essence is My love, which never falters. Trust deeply and completely in this simple, divine truth and be at peace.

NATURE'S JOY

Speaking of joy, have you ever noticed that Mother Earth's expressions of joy are scattered all around her? Have you ever thought that a tree's leaves, a flower's beauty, a rushing waterfall, a burbling stream, a wave hitting the shore, a mountain peak covered in a crown of snow, a dandelion in the middle of an expanse of perfectly green grass, a weed popping up through a crack in a sidewalk, a hummingbird's flight, the screech of a hawk, the clouds scuttling across the sky are all expressions of Mother Nature's joy?

If you accepted this premise, would you ever look at Mother Earth the same way again?

YOU ARE NOT FORSAKEN

There will be times when it feels as if I have forsaken the world. Nothing, My Dear, could be farther from the truth. I will never abandon you. I am always present in every experience.

It's true, however, that even when you are intimately connected with Me, challenges will still occur. This is because you are part of a larger collective of souls who are all on their own unique path and all the while entangled within the greater human experience. Therefore, problems requiring solutions do not mean you did something wrong, that you have somehow angered or upset Me. I could never be angry with you. You could never upset Me. I could never see you as less than perfect. Situations that you do not prefer are simply part of being human at this stage in your evolution.

There is something you can do, however, to make this all seem much easier. You tend to turn to Me when life gets pretty rocky. It might help to know that when things are unusually difficult, I am leading you to your greatest potential. Still, the more you turn to Me in moments of joy, or even in simple day-to-day ordinariness, these uncomfortable occasions will become fewer and farther between. Soon, you will begin to notice that any troublesome predicaments that come your way are much more easily navigated.

When you consistently connect with Me on a daily basis and you steadfastly trust this connection, tough circumstances will feel much less daunting and you will know without a doubt that *this too shall pass*. You will trust that I have your back as you walk your way through it. Eventually, it will all feel quite manageable and sometimes, even rather silly.

The truth is, when you truly trust in My presence in all things, you can meet even the most taxing condition in peace, love and forgiveness. There is much more we can say about this, especially around those experiences that are traumatic to a human soul, but know that this is possible. Know that there are other humans that have walked your planet who have accomplished this. Know that as all are created in My image, they are no more special than you. As Jesus the Christed One has said, '*You can do this and more.*'

Certainly reach for Me when times are hard, and also get used to reaching for Me in those ordinary, day-to-day, life-is-going-well times, too. Touch base with me each day, even for a few moments. As you do this, know that when things are rough, feeling My love, hearing My guidance and trusting your path will get easier and easier to do.

STAR DUST

Do you ever contemplate star dust? You may want to try it sometime, for if you do, you will find the essence of Me, and of you, within the trillions-year-old detritus of a once brilliantly shining radiance.

For you see, My love is what holds it all together and no matter what condition an object appears to be in, My love remains strong within it. It is always vibrant and alive. This means that even when you are at your worst, even in the hardest moments, *you* are still vibrant, alive and filled with My love.

Know that as you hold an intention to touch this vibrant, living love, no matter the circumstances, you can and you will.

LAUGHTER

What is it about laughter? Have you ever pondered why humans laugh? We've talked a little about how important the heart is in regard to love, but have you ever stopped to check in with your heart when you are laughing or when you hear another laugh?

Joy and love are very close cousins when it comes to the world of human emotion. Joy is the rush of emotion you get when you feel the no-holds-barred love that is Me, and laughter is your body's physical response to being present to so much joy and so much love.

It is interesting to pay attention to the different nuances within your body to laughter, depending upon what triggers it. You will notice, for example, that it is less genuine at a sitcom than when your child is giggling so much their entire body is doubled over. You will sense that your laughter at a sarcastic joke, which is often at the expense of another person, feels more constricting than your delight at watching a dolphin propel out of the water, twist and dive back under. Laughter inspired by the natural world, which includes being in the presence of others laughing, is almost always more open and expansive than that of the unnatural world.

Observe that when you really laugh, your chest puffs out, your heart swells and you feel wide open. This is you, knowing the expansiveness of Me. This is because, for an instant, you are unguarded and completely in the moment. You are *in love* with the moment. Now we have come full circle. Laughter is a by-product of joy which is derived from being very present to My love.

Now, if you aren't experiencing laughter, if you really have to try hard to create an opportunity to laugh, well this is another conversation entirely, is it not?

FREE WILL

You have been given free will because I want to watch you play and create and experiment and experience through your choices and circumstances. I want you to choose. I want you to prefer. I want you to dream and desire. This is how I expand, explore, sense and participate in My own consciousness.

Understand that I will not punish you if you use it unwisely for that would be a bit nonsensical of Me. Certainly some choices will appear to be more loving than others but in My book, choice is simply choice. I don't view things in the way that humans do—good and bad, right and wrong, up and down, left and right, black and white. I see everything as an opportunity to experience something new.

Still, if making up your mind is in some way difficult, I am always here. You always have a direct connection to Me and truly, all you need do is ask and you shall receive. The counsel I offer can come in many forms—a random desire for something, a number that keeps popping up seemingly by chance, a particular chapter or paragraph in a book that an acquaintance recommends, really good advice from a friend.

But the most potent way to receive My guidance is to sit quietly and listen for that whisper of a voice inside of you that offers understanding and direction. You will know it is Me by the way the information feels. While what comes to you may seem to be irrational or illogical when measured against societal norms, when you sit with it and sense it in your gut, you will simply know it to be true.

Of course by definition, you can ignore it without any judgment from Me. I will love you no matter your choices. I will love you whether or not you consult My guidance and whether or not you follow it. I will love you whether your actions are loving or less than loving. I will love you no matter what you do because I love you for who you ARE, I love you for the all of you, and nothing you could ever do will change this.

In essence, human free will is My gift to Myself. So choose and choose and choose again and consult Me or don't, but know that I am always, always here cheering you on, reveling in those choices. Never doubt that in you I am well pleased.

ROMANTIC LOVE

Let's talk about romantic love for a moment. Some cultures suggest there is one person who completes you and one person whom you complete. Jerry McGuire notwithstanding, this is not a notion of intimate partnership that is the highest form of service, for you could never complete another nor could another ever complete you. You are already whole. You are already perfect in My eyes.

What you actually yearn to experience is to merge with another in order to amplify love. Amplification is an interesting word. It is no longer well used, though at one time this term was an embedded concept within certain societies. Ultimately, it is not the goal to better each other but rather to expand love in such a way that it is felt throughout the cosmos. This kind of intimate union is what a sacred loving partnership is meant to be.

Know, too, that while procreation can be a by-product of such a coupling, it is not the end goal. However, when a child is conceived within such a union, that child will only expand that love even further and so on, and so on, and so on.

While I am neither judging nor condemning mates that do not hold this highest of intentions, I am suggesting that ultimately, it is the pinnacle of what humans in loving connection are capable of.

Jerry Maguire (film, 1996)

ONLY NOW

Those of you that are consciously walking your evolutionary path sometimes think that you are behind, that you should have accomplished more by now and thus that you are failing somehow. When you experience situations that are hard, you can feel as if you have chosen unwisely and therefore, slowed your progress. You can feel bad about yourself because of these thoughts that you harbor but please do not think any of this is true.

When you face great challenge, it means that you are trusted to be of great service through certain aspects of your soul that you have brought with you to this lifetime, no matter the current circumstances in which you find yourself. And if things take a little longer than you hoped, be reassured that the universe is rearranging itself to fit what is in perfect alignment. Keep in mind that ultimately, there is no ahead, there is no behind... there is only right now.

At any given moment, you truly have no idea the level of service you are living, the impact you are having, or the level of service and impact yet to come. Understand that whether or not you are *doing* something purposeful, you are still having an effect that is immeasurable through your Beingness. Remember, too, that whole free will thing. You are always loved and trusted to live out your service in whatever way you choose and I am always here walking beside you, ensuring that you have what you need for your inevitable and always trending evolution.

Hold up your head. Stand proud. Be at peace with who you are.

FIERCE LOVE

Love yourself fiercely wherever you are. Accept and allow whatever is happening. Be who you choose to be as often as possible. It is all okay.

UNBREAKABLE

Can you trust yourself so much that you can be in peace, love and joy no matter the external circumstances? Can you relax into this as your natural state? Can you embrace the notion that you never have to consider your own value because you simply know who you are in My eyes? Can you relax into an ease and flow in all that you do because you trust and love yourself so completely?

Can you be unshakeable, unbreakable, invincible within your great big huge open heart?

VALIDATION

Do you reach out for validation from others? Do you need others to confirm your goodness or your worth?

It is lonely being human sometimes. Part of why you look for validation outside of yourself is because it is comforting to receive evidence of your worthiness from another soul. Yet what if the proof you seek comes from sitting with your own heart? What if it is *this* connection that provides you with all of the wisdom, all of the answers, all of the support and all of the confirmation you ever need? Who would you be then?

Try this out. When you yearn for companionship, wisdom or validation from others, sit with your heart open in the most expansive way and the intention of finding what it is you are seeking through that open-hearted connection with Me. Get used to finding anything you think you need *in here*, rather than *out there*. The more you do this, the easier it will become and the richer the experience.

The peace that passeth all understanding is within you; it is within your grasp.

CLEAN SLATE

What if you could offer yourself the grace of a clean slate? What if you could just be in the moment, trusting who you are right now, rather than judging your actions in the past? What does this level of grace feel like when you grant it to yourself? Does it look and feel like freedom? Like peace? Like love?

This kind of grace, directed at the self, is a level of mastery that few humans achieve and it is yours, should you choose it.

BE LOVE

You are here, at this place, in this time to anchor love and light into the world. Simply be that love and light as often as you can.

Everything else you do pales in comparison. This is your true mission. You will grow into it. Grant yourself compassion if you are not there yet. Forgive yourself when you step away from it momentarily and then return to it once again.

Know yourself as the love and light of Me that flows through everything, that flows through you. Keep expanding into this knowing of yourself as love and light and all else will follow.

HEARTACHE

We have talked about My presence within your physical body, residing within your heart space.

So what does it mean if you are diagnosed with a heart condition? What if you have what your doctors call a heart attack or heart failure? Does this mean that somehow you are not a loving person, that in some way you are not worthy of love? Generally speaking, when someone has heart 'disease', it means that they hold so much love for humanity, they have taken on the suffering of others to an extent that the heart becomes overwhelmed. Some souls come into a lifetime with the weight of the world on their heart. You know them to be angels on Earth, even as their physical bodies struggle under that weight. Those who have a heart attack often carry a different weight—the weight of anger, despair and underneath, a deep sadness that attacks their ability to love others and themselves fully.

    Dear One, do not take your heart for granted. Many of you never give a moment's notice to this miracle of love that is accessible in every moment but I am here, right here, and this beating, pulsing, living powerhouse of love is always reminding you that this is so.

COSMIC COLLABORATION

You have been told that I am almighty and while this is essentially accurate, what has gotten lost in translation is that, in this Earthly experiment, you are made in My image.

Through free will, I have given *you* a great deal of power and control and essentially placed myself in the role of your aide de camp, your virtual assistant. We are collaborators, you and I. I love and trust you so much that I gave you the urge to create, the ability to choose and the tools to construct your unique existence. You get to dream, set intentions, make choices and take actions and through your clarity (the clearer and bolder the better), I get my marching orders. Life is what *you* make of it when you consciously use the free will you have been gifted.

I urge you to stop looking so much *out there* at your external environment to determine your reality; dare to create your own. First, ask yourself some questions. What kind of world do I want to experience? What fulfills me? What brings me joy? What brings me peace? Where do I choose to focus my attention? What feels true for me? What do I want to bring to the planet? What is the boldest vision I have for myself? Truly, I have given you the wheel to steer yourself in the direction your answers lead you. I have set it up so that you can live a life of peace, joy, abundance and love despite what appears to be going on around you. This is the truth of you.

Now, if sometimes what shows up in your life isn't exactly what you envision, have faith. I promise there is something there for you to discover that will make your ultimate destination even sweeter. Continue to state your intentions, focus your attention, take hold and aim true. I am here, clearing the way and paving new paths when a road is blocked. I am bringing you sustenance for the journey in a myriad of ways. Believe in yourself. Trust in My love for you. Together, we are making your dreams come true.

HOLI-DAYS

Have you ever wondered why you have holidays/holy days that, in addition to religious tradition, include mythical figures blessed with magical powers—Santa Claus, the Easter Bunny, Halloween, the Tooth Fairy? Have you thought about why sacred dates such as the day Christ is born, the day Christ arose, the day of the dead, and even the day you lose a tooth have become affiliated with made up, magical figures focused on giving gifts and treats? Have you ever considered what you are actually going for here?

You are trying to capture, in your Earthly reality, an essence that has been lost but is nonetheless so quintessential to the human psyche, you simply could not abide in its absence. What is this fundamental aspect of life that you are missing so badly? My children, *you are missing your own magic*.

YOU are Santa Claus. YOU are the Easter Bunny. YOU are the ghost and the goblin and the witch and the dancing skeleton. YOU are the Tooth Fairy. You are the magic that you seek—you have simply forgotten this is so. Through these powerful characters that you have created from your imaginations, you are reminding yourselves that you are prolific and potent manifestors. You are reminding yourselves that giving and receiving and abundance and prosperity are natural states of being human. You are reminding yourselves that space and time are man-made conceptions that can be bent to your will. You are reminding yourselves that something lost is a gateway to regeneration. You are reminding yourselves that death is not the end of the story. You are reminding yourselves how it feels to be light-hearted and free. You are reminding yourselves that through Me, the cosmos is infinitely bountiful and you are a living fractal of that cosmos. You are reminding yourselves that anything is possible.

When you remember who you are, you have no further need of mythical figures or special days of the year set apart from the ordinary ones. You will know time and density to be the human constructs they truly are. You will know that you can be in two places, or a million places, at once. You will know that you are infinite and death is just an illusion. You will know yourself to be that fractal of Me, filled with wonder, generosity, joy, gratitude and love in each and every now moment. You will know that you are magic and every day is holy.

SOUL CONNECTION

People are not always meant to stay in your life. Sometimes others show up briefly in order to share some wisdom, provide some much needed comic relief or reflect something back to you that you may want to take a look at for your own growth. Sometimes they are connectors—someone who appears merely to introduce you to someone else that will be important to you. Sometimes they arrive to propel you into something completely new. People can show up in any number of iterations and their length of stay is not an indication of their importance to you.

Know, though, that if they do not remain in your life for as long as you hoped, even if they exit under circumstances that cause you to feel lost and wounded, it does not mean that anything about that relationship was a mistake. If it happened, it was meant to be. If them leaving or coming into your life was difficult in any way, see if you can find your way to gratitude for what they ultimately offered you, even if the coming or the going was painful. The people who impact us the most, whether that impact feels beautiful or very, very hard, are always of the greatest service to us.

As souls, you come with an intention that is loving and positive, even if the way it works out in a human lifetime doesn't feel as such. If you can't find gratitude for all those who enter your life, see if you can at least acknowledge a positive *soul* intention. See if you can at least accept that some new seed might have sprung from the ashes. *See if you can at least love the soul and forgive the human* because in the end (and in the beginning), it is all an offering of love.

BIRTH & DEATH

Shall we talk about birth and death? It is hard to find another experience that has a greater influence on a human than the birth or death of a beloved.

You often wonder where you will go when you die but have you wondered where you came from before you were born? It is hard for many of you to imagine but they are, in at least one respect, exactly the same process—going from formless light to a human form and going from human form to formless light. In both instances, you are the energy of Me that runs through all things and you are also You. This is a cosmic paradox, to be equally one with Me and uniquely you.

Your soul, the essence of you, remains always whether or not it dwells in human form or some other form. You, the essence of you, never dies. You, the essence of you, always lives even after the form that you take in each life expression, what you call a body, is no longer. The essence of you is the essence of Me, albeit with a certain uniqueness that is stunning in its beauty.

When a child is born, a soul lit from within comes into form to experience their singular beauty. When a person dies, a soul merges back into the love and light that births all creation. Know that each and every birth, each and every death, is a celebration of the greatest magnitude.

ANGELS

Do you ever think about angels? When speaking about love, we simply cannot ignore the role they play. There are many orders of angels but they all exist with the highest calling—to hold unconditional love for humans.

As angels hold space for that unconditional love, they are also at your disposal to assist you with all manner of things. They are incredibly happy to bring more ease into your life as their aid often inspires gratitude and gratitude is a gateway to love. Through their interventions, love grows and expands in the world.

While they are always nearby, waiting to serve you, they do require an invitation. You must directly ask them for their help. Now, this doesn't mean that you can ask them to support you in acquiring things just for the sake of acquiring. For example, let's say you want a new car because you are tired of your existing model and saw something brand new that you would love to have. Well, this is not a job for an angel. However, let's say you live paycheck to paycheck and you absolutely depend upon your car to get you back and forth to your workplace. If there were a problem with the mechanics of your current car, the dominoes might fall, creating very hard times. Calling upon your angels to keep your car running in prime condition or to bring better, more reliable transportation into your life, IS the perfect mission.

If you haven't made it a habit to request your angels' guidance, you might begin to make this a daily practice. Request their support to keep your life flowing smoothly in some important way, raise your consciousness or deliver patience as you deal with certain people or situations. Ask for whatever it is that would bring you more peace with a sincere desire and a knowing that you are heard and acknowledged.

You may trust that your angels are with you—this is the role they have accepted, to wait in the wings (pun intended) until they are needed. When you consistently collaborate with them, you will receive unimaginable gifts, experience the wonder and mystery of infinite possibility and experience a love so pure, you will know Me.

Your angels await.

JUST RIGHT

Your love for Me is always just right but if there is ever a time when you believe it isn't enough in your eyes, know that I've got more than enough for the both of us. Never worry that you are lacking in any way. You are always just you being you and you are always perfect in My eyes. When you trust this, you will be at peace in every now moment.

DIVINE ORCHESTRATION

Life is a deep, rich, complex symphony that never ends. Don't try to compose it; just allow the music to carry you, flowing with every note. Revel in its depth, its beauty, its luster and its mystery. Let the divine orchestration of you unfold in all of its magnificent, intricate perfection.

LOVE & PUNISHMENT

I am asked a lot if people who do bad things deserve love. I say to you that they deserve the most love of all because for a human to conduct an act of violence, abuse or betrayal, these acts can only come from one who was not loved enough.

Sending love to another is one of the greatest acts of service. When groups of humans gather for this 'soul' purpose, it can have an astonishing impact. Hate is not the answer. Punishment is not the answer. Violence to combat violence is not the answer. Love is the only answer to anything that comes from an absence of love.

Please know that you get to keep yourself safe by setting boundaries. You do not have to put yourself in close proximity to someone in order to love them; you can sit with the intention of sending love to another through the ether and I assure you, it will be received.

When you can offer love to someone that does not appear on the surface to be deserving, you have reached a level of mastery. This is wisdom that all masters who have walked an Earthly timeline have attempted to share and how all masters have attempted to live. This you can do, too, if you choose. When you do, you help transform any and all savagery that exists on your planet.

Choosing is your greatest human gift and your greatest responsibility. Are you willing to choose love?

A BIGGER PICTURE

Do you ever want something so badly that you ask Me to help you get it, only to have it not show up at all? Or perhaps, to have it show up in a different fashion than what you were hoping? Have you ever felt that I was displeased with you for some reason, as a result?

I tell you this, I am never displeased with you. When something you desire doesn't arrive, please know that it is merely because I see a bigger picture and I have more expansive plans for you than you could ever imagine. I am always most concerned for your overall well-being and the well-being of all others, and sometimes this means that what you think you want isn't the thing that is going to carry you to the greatest version of the grandest vision I have for you. I see all aspects of you. I know your past and future (though ultimately, time is of no consequence and all facets of you are happening simultaneously). I know the pure love that you are and the magnificence of you; therefore, I am always bringing you the people, places, opportunities and things that will aid you in becoming your greatest, grandest, most expansive, most magnificent self.

It would assist Me ever so much if you could trust Me, if you trust what arrives as divine. You certainly don't have to do so, but it would help your journey go much more smoothly. Either way, your destination is assured.

CREATIVE GENIUS

Whose approval are you seeking? Why do you seek it? What kind of validation do you hope to gain? Could you see a time that has you only ever seeking those things from yourself about yourself? Truly, this is where you are going.

You have a unique gift and mission, as does every other human. What good would it do, then, to search for anything outside of yourself? No one knows who you are and what you are here to do better than you do. *You are here to be someone that only you can be.*

Your experiences, your thoughts, your beliefs and your perceptions of the world and your place in it are meant to collide with your unique creative genius in order to evolve into a dazzling work of art that is your authentic life. I know that, given how the world works today, this might seem impossible but it is only impossible if you seek to know yourself through anything outside of yourself.

Your true purpose in this lifetime is to first know yourself so well, so intimately, that you are in touch with your own uniqueness and then to trust yourself enough to birth a life from it. Know what you love, what you prefer, what makes you sing with joy, what brings you peace and go do that in whatever way you can, each and every day. This is why you have come to be an embodied soul. Your divine calling can only be found inside of you; only you can know its truth.

PURE LOVE

Humans have been taught that love has many facets, that friendship love is different from love for a child or love for a romantic partner or love for one's work. On one level this can seem true, yet it is helpful to know that on the grandest, most cosmic level, there is one love that flows through all things, one love that creates all things, one love that is everywhere all at once. That one love holds the highest frequency, a vibration of sound and light that is at the core of everything.

Ultimately, it is not love that has different facets, it is you that perceives different aspects of love depending upon the openness of your heart, the evolution of your consciousness, and the frequency that you hold. Every human has the capacity to feel this core, cosmic love that is undifferentiated. It simply is.

You will always have the opportunity to experience yourself within what seems to be an aspect of love, yet when you hold an intention of feeling the greatest love imaginable in all things, you will begin to have *that* experience. Try sitting with yourself in quiet meditation, eyes closed, with the intention of experiencing My love in its highest form. Focus on opening your heart. Don't overthink this—be out of your mind and in your heart. See what happens. Know that as you become good at this, you can carry that feeling with you, and when you do, you are a pure conduit of that love.

Notice as you carry this love out into the world, how people respond to you. Notice the lightness in the faces of others, in the energy of those conversations and in the energies you feel swirling around you. If you do this more and more, you can cure any addiction by replacing it—whether it's food or booze or drugs or sex or work or power or greed—with the high you get from being that pure conduit of love. You do not have to be a saint or a guru or a philosopher or especially educated in any way to do this. You simply have to hold the intention, and practice, until it becomes second nature.

You don't even have to tell anyone w*hat you are being*. In fact, you will find that it's much more fun to keep it to yourself. Simply revel in the magic that unfolds.

TRUTH

Many humans, even those who know themselves to be on the spiritual path, feel that seeking the truth is the way into My heart. This is understandable, but also misguided.

Truth is a very nebulous thing. There are very few truths and only one frequency of My heart and that is love and love's manifestations of peace, joy, compassion, grace, forgiveness and gratitude. If you do not hold these things for another, as well as for yourself, you are not experiencing truth.

Be very careful of anything that is presented to you as true. I say to you, if something is presented to you as truth and it shames, blames, punishes, humiliates or wars with another, it is most certainly not. Any truth that presents itself as such, but does not reflect love, cannot be authentic.

Here is a better idea. Instead of seeking truth, seek love.

RIGHT HERE

Where are you putting your attention? Most humans place their attention either on what has occurred in the past or what might occur in the future. It breaks My heart to know this, for when you spend so much time in the past and future, you miss out on the experience of love in its highest form.

While a memory of love might be found in the past and a desire for love might be found in the future, genuine love can only be found in the present.

Focus your attention in the right here, right now and you shall encounter a more divine state of love.

MOTHER MOON

The moon has many purposes, some of which you have discovered and some of which you have not. One of her most intimate reasons for being is so you can feel less alone.

She is a soothing presence, is she not? Her soft glow feels nurturing and full of promise and somehow so intimate, like she is there just for you, like she knows your secrets and is rooting you on. And this is all true. Your Earth, your moon, your sun and all of the other planets, moons and suns in the cosmos have a consciousness, an intelligence.

You can trust what you feel about her, your moon. She is a most loving presence meant, in part, to help you remember that you are loved and cherished, that you matter. As your Shakespeare once said, '*There are more things in heaven and earth, Horatio...*' The moon is here to remind you that magic exists, that you are someone special, and that there is a motherly presence lighting your way, even in the darkness.

PLAGUE

There are times when it is difficult to believe in anything. There are times when it all seems to have gone wrong, when life seems completely off kilter. What do you do when these times plague you? For it does feel like a plague, does it not? It feels as if something has entered your bloodstream, your *life* stream, and steered it in a direction that makes absolutely no sense, that has nothing to do with who you are or what you want.

Ah, but these are the times that precede great breakthroughs in consciousness and faith. These are the times when the cure for what ails you arrives. These are the times that precede change, transformation and the opportunity to not only live differently but with more love, peace, gratitude and joy.

When you experience a plague, or any crisis for that matter, what is important often becomes infinitely clear. Crisis steers you towards clarity and ultimately, clarity is what you want because it is what drives true change, the kind that is in your best and highest good. In everyday life, however, it can be hard to find. Sometimes it is because we are addicted to the way things are. We know we must change but the idea of change seems too painful. Sometimes there are too many choices; life presents us with too many shiny things to be chased. In either case, a plague comes to help you notice that there is often really only the choice between one thing or another. Sometimes crisis is the only place that makes those two things stand out in base relief.

If you are in the midst of a crisis of faith, see if there is, under all the detritus, a very simple choice to be made, something that is so stark, so obvious that there is no doubt which thing you will choose. Generally, the choice is between two polar opposites. Use your clarity around this choice to drive your next decisions, your next creations, your next steps and you will set the change in motion that will send the plague packing.

Often, the bedrock of any choice is simply whether you trust Me or whether you don't. Paradoxically, this is usually both the simplest and the hardest choice you can make. You can trust Me, but will you? Please know that if you choose to place your trust elsewhere, it matters not to Me. I am always here, cheering you on, supporting you in any way I can.

OUT OF YOUR MIND

Have you ever been out of your mind? It is fascinating to Me that this has been taught as being a bad thing. To be out of your mind is not seen as a particularly good thing, yet love will not be found in the mind.

~

*Have the courage to lose your mind
in order to find your heart.*

PRESENCE

Presence—you feel that even if the idea of presence is elegantly simple, the execution isn't, because staying in each moment, without a glance back to the past or forward to the future, seems not just daunting but impossible.

Actually, being present is pretty basic; you make the decision to be so and then practice it until it is second nature. Once the decision is made and your intention is set, it is very doable.

I will also share that it is worth it. Decide to be present without story, without casting backward to lean on previous experience or forward in an attempt to know an unknown future, and stay in a state of love, joy, gratitude or peace.

If you all do this, it will bring every one of you home.

SUFFERING

Suffering is something every human experiences. But why, you ask? Would it surprise you to know that the main job of suffering is to lead you to love?

Suffering and love don't seem to have anything to do with one another, at least intellectually. Yet I tell you that they are inextricably linked, for suffering is one of the few things that can show you where love appears to be absent, whether in relationship with another or with yourself. Suffering *is* love, albeit in a form you may have never considered.

There is much talk about enlightenment but most of you want enlightenment to be like a switch that is flipped and just like that, you are an enlightened being. Certainly, there have been some masters that have become enlightened in this way, but it is not typical. For most of you, it is a journey and suffering is one of the vehicles that transports you on the path. There are few things that can propel someone forward in their spiritual evolution quite like suffering.

Suffering is an enormous clue—one that is hard to miss—to any perceived lack of love and its cousins, peace and joy. Truly, when you pull the thread of your suffering it can lead you back to love. The next time you become aware that you are suffering, even if it is over something small, ask yourself, '*What does this suffering tell me about where I might be lacking love and where I might need to return to love?*' Keep asking with compassion for yourself and all others. Follow your intuition. Forgive, if it is required. Take any action you are called to take. Do this until your suffering has been replaced by the love that now fills the space it once occupied in your life and in your heart. If you can do this consistently, you are approaching a level of mastery that few humans have achieved.

I promise you that if you use suffering in this way, it will change the way you think about it, and yourself, and you will be well on your way to embodying your own divinity.

YOUR HIGHEST CALLING

When you see a problem in the world, something you believe must be fixed or healed or changed in any way, focus on your internal, your eternal light. This is your greatest gift to humankind.

Your ego will tell you this is ridiculous. It will say, *'I have to DO something. I should fight, contribute, donate, protest, cry out, loudly proclaim how I feel, invent a solution, DO SOMETHING!'* If you choose to do any of these things, that is wonderful, just know that it is not your highest calling.

Love is the balm for every wound in your world—every problem, every challenge, every act of violence, every act of sabotage and betrayal, every illness, every act of destruction.

Be love. Be the greatest, grandest, most all-encompassing version of that love. Spill it out into the world. Feel yourself as that perfect, brilliant, sparkling diamond dissolving into the sparkling, brilliant, effervescent light that is everywhere, that is everything, that is Me, that is You.

LOVE + TRUST = PEACE

What is peace, exactly and how do we get there?

Peace is a feeling of total contentment born from a complete love and acceptance of everything in your current awareness in each and every now moment. True peace requires a combination of presence and surrender to what is—no story, no judgment.

You cannot achieve this level of peace unless you love and trust yourself and love and trust Me. You wouldn't think loving and trusting yourself would be so important to being at peace, yet I can assure you, loving and trusting Me without loving and trusting yourself will only get you halfway.

Why might this be so? A wifi signal is a good analogy. You need it to run both ways. You need the signal that is sent out to be received and you need that received signal to be returned. You need a continuous feedback loop of electromagnetic waves. Without that, you might put something out into the universe but you will never know it reached its intended target, and vice versa.

You and Me, we are that wifi feedback loop and trust is our electromagnetic wave, our frequency. You must trust yourself so that you trust your connection with Me. Otherwise, you will spend much of your time second guessing. To be at peace with everything means a no-doubt trust in yourself so that you have a no-doubt trust in our connection. If you doubt yourself, somewhere along the way, you will doubt Me, too.

Love and trust go hand in hand. You can easily imagine trying to trust someone you don't like very much and how hard that might be, especially if it involves trusting your life with that person. On the flip side, isn't it so much easier to trust someone that you love? Well, this is what we are talking about, isn't it? We are talking about putting your life into our joined hands, are we not? This requires an enormous amount of trust because I can assure you that, for a variety of reasons, there will always be things that show up in your life that you won't necessarily prefer.

This level of trust—that allows you to accept and surrender to everything that arrives in your life—requires a love so deep that it is without question.

All I ask of you is this—if you come to understand that what I am saying here feels true to you, begin to love and trust yourself right now, right here, today and know peace.

LITTLE REMINDER

Just a little reminder... I love you.

THE LOVE YOU SEEK

Your world, even in all of its chaotic messiness, in all of its pain and sorrow and suffering, contains so much love. Can you see it? Can you touch it? Can you sense it? Can you Be it?

I tell you, Dear One, it is here because YOU are here. Be the love you seek. It will come back to you. Dare to be in the spiral of love.

DIAMOND LIGHT

You are a brilliant diamond, formed under the pressure of being human. You have been shaped and molded by time, emotion, circumstances and yet you are always, in all ways, that dazzling diamond light throughout the eons.

You may think of yourself at times as a simple rock without luster, without depth, without clarity. I tell you now, you always shine brightly in My eyes. You have always been, and will always be, a perfect, radiant, luminous jewel. Never doubt this.

OSMOSIS

Love can be shared with another simply by being in their vicinity. Did you know this? Did you know that others can experience your love as it seeps into their bloodstream through the chemical makeup of the human body via osmosis? The human body is mostly water and water holds an intelligence, a consciousness, that picks up on the frequency of emotion. Unfortunately, emotions like fear and anger work this way, too. This is why you sometimes meet up with someone and can't wait to get away from them. You can feel their emotions, through this process of osmosis, within your own body.

It is helpful to know that when you hold a frequency, it goes out into the ether—into the soil and the birds and the trees and the food you cook and anything else that also holds the consciousness of water. Be mindful of the energy that you are putting out into the world based upon how you are feeling. Be aware that it is not only you that is affected—all other living things are affected, too. Do not lament. This is actually a GOOD thing! It means that you can make a huge impact in the world around you just by focusing on love.

You can always start by sitting quietly and tapping into My love. Simply ask,

'God, let me feel your love.'

Then breathe slowly and rhythmically. Do this whenever you have a few moments. Do this whenever you are feeling less than loved, or less than loving. When you are filled with love, go out and share it. Let it flow out into the world.

'Let my love be with you.'

LOVE OF CHRIST

For the love of Christ... Some humans say this as a roar of emotion when something doesn't go their way. It is actually a blessing that has been turned, over time, into a mixture of prayer (as in, please help me) and dismay (I can't believe this just happened). For the love of Christ, let us try to get back some semblance of what this phrase was initially meant to convey.

Who is, what is, Christ? It may surprise you to learn that Christ is a level of consciousness, rather than a person. Christ consciousness is essentially My unconditional love carried into matter, into form. Love is a frequency; it is the frequency that runs through all things. Christians call Jesus '*the Christ*' and yet Jesus is not the Christ so much as the one who fully embodied this consciousness continuously.

You may have heard that Jesus said, '*You are made in My image*' and '*You too shall do these things and more'*, and these expressions allude to the idea that you, too, can embody that level of consciousness that carries the seed of My love and plants it everywhere you go. Like Jesus, you will embody Christ consciousness when you have dialed into this frequency nonstop, when you are locked in. Christ consciousness allows you to simply be with everything and resonate with it all. It is true that you have the capacity to achieve this level of consciousness; you can, and assuredly in some expression of your soul, you shall.

When you achieve Christ consciousness, living this way as a human brings the solutions, opportunities and potentials that resonate with you, uniquely. In fact, they come so easily, so effortlessly that you can feel a bit guilty about it all because it is quite magical. You simply carry the frequency of love for all things with you in every moment, every where. You simply float in that sea of love.

Do what you do, be who you are *'for the love of Christ'*.

RECLAIM YOURSELF

If there is anything you are holding onto that lessens, restricts or diminishes your love for yourself, or the way you value yourself, this is something you will want to address head on. If it feels uncomfortable emotionally, know that your discomfort is leading you to some kind of realization or action that will ultimately bring you to more peace and more love.

Challenging emotions such as fear, restriction, anger, jealousy, frustration and sadness are clues that something is amiss, that your energy is being siphoned off somehow. Acknowledging and honoring them is powerful. Trust your instincts in terms of what is happening and what you need in order to tip the scales in your favor. Is there another human in your life that doesn't have your best interests at heart? Is there some situation where you are handing over your power, your desires or your value to another?

Strive to bring self love, self worth and self trust back into balance, whether this means speaking your truth, setting a boundary or even walking away. Trust that, as you reclaim your self love and self worth, you are opening the door for all others to do the same. Caring for yourself in this way is a radically loving, radically healing act.

DISLIKE

Did you know that you do not have to like another to truly love them? This is a paradox worth sinking your teeth into.

There are people on your planet with whom you struggle to be with. This is part of your personal sovereignty and it is to be respected and honored. Yet the soul of that other person is also to be respected and honored; they have come into their own Earth-body to live out certain aspects of the human condition, just like you. As you sit with this understanding, even if you cannot honor and respect those aspects they chose in this life expression to explore, then perhaps you can more easily acknowledge and celebrate their courage. As you likely know well, being human oftentimes takes guts and determination.

Yet I tell you a secret… typically, the aspects that move you to not want to spend time with another are aspects you will find within your own countenance, albeit in a slightly different way. I urge you to open your heart and visualize this person. See what causes you distress and then look for that very same thing within you. Find the grace of compassion and forgiveness for you and them because forgiveness and compassion transmute anything back to love. Know that all is well.

STORIES

You have made your world out to be such a complicated place.

Part of the issue here is that as your human intellect has grown more complex, so have your stories. It helps to recognize them for exactly what they are. You assign the meaning that accompanies every circumstance; this is why two people, or ten, can share the same situation or reside in the same family and have very different perspectives on what is taking place at any given time.

The great news is, I gave you the power to change a drama into a comedy, nonfiction into fiction or prose into poetry. You are in charge of your thoughts, beliefs, values and actions. You decide if you're the superhero or the villain, the success or the failure, the beauty or the beast. Ultimately, you can decide to drop the need to tell a tale altogether. You can live your experience, be in the moment and refuse to judge any of it. You have a term for this state of being—enlightenment—because you are indeed living *lightly*, without the heaviness of judgment, negativity or victimhood.

I see the good in everything—all of your hopes and dreams, your pain and fear and anger. I hold no definition of good or bad, right or wrong. It is all beautiful to me. It is all experience within the spectrum of love. Be in the moment. Live your experience. Do not judge it. This is how the world becomes simple once again.

PRACTICE LOVE

Love begets more love. This is not only a Universal, but a Cosmic truth.

Love resides in everything, everywhere and like the rain that raises the level of a body of water, your love raises the level of love in every thing, every where. As you love yourself more, you raise the level of love. As you love another more, you raise the level of love. As you appreciate your possessions and lovingly care for them, you raise the level of love. As you collaborate with Mother Earth in loving co-creation, you raise the level of love.

There is a practice, should you opt to work with it, that goes something like this. Sit or lie down in a comfortable position. Breathe easily and rhythmically until you find yourself at peace, with your mind quiet. Then focus on your heart complex within your chest; keep breathing and notice when it feels open and expansive. When you achieve this state, breathe Me into your heart upon the inhale and as you exhale, send all of that energy out into the world.

This exercise will look and feel a little different for everyone. Don't let your mind get in the way; simply be with it. If you feel peaceful, energized or expansive as you finish, you know you have done well. Choosing to expand the love within you and to send it out to be amplified and shared is a huge gift to the world and its impact cannot be underestimated.

You may also adopt a prayer, along these lines, to be said daily, '*God, as your Holy Child, allow me to give and receive love today.*' Say this upon awakening and see what happens.

Always remember, love begets more love.

GRANDEST VISION

What would it mean to live the greatest version of the grandest vision I could ever hold for you? What might your life look like if you held this intention, prayed this prayer, every day? Where do you think life would take you then?

BE PEACE, BE LOVE

It is far easier to be at peace with the world when you are at peace with yourself.

It is far easier to be in love with the world when you are in love with yourself.

STOP, LOOK, LISTEN

Stop, look and listen. If you are of a certain age, you will remember this direction given to youngsters to help them be safe in moments of possible danger. While this advice has gone out of fashion, I would like to bring it back, for it is excellent guidance, though I would like to put a new spin on it.

When you are in conversation with another, whether it is your partner, spouse, child, friend, co-worker, supervisor, cashier at the grocery store or wait staff at a restaurant, think about this very simple instruction. Stop your thoughts. Stop your mind from thinking. Look into the person's eyes you are conversing with. Listen, really listen to what they are saying. Then, take one breath before you respond.

I would offer to you that doing this routinely will change the very nature of all of your conversations in some very surprising ways because it is an act of love. It is an act of love because it allows you to be in the moment with that other, to really see and hear them, and to also be in the moment when you respond, which opens you up to the richness of wisdom, insight and clarity that only comes when one is calm and present. This is one of the best ways to BE loving with everyone you meet. Try this on for size and see if it fits.

REMEMBER

What would the world be like if every single one of you knew you were infinitely lovable and loved to infinity? How would you treat each other? How would you care for each other? How would you choose to spread that love around?

The way that humans love today is but a fraction of the love that runs through the universe. Most often, the love you experience as a human being is but a tiny sliver, an 'amuse-bouche' of the love that is available to you. My darlings, you have no idea what awaits you, what is available to you, what is possible to experience.

How do you embody this kind of love, a love that is so mighty it brings light to every atom of darkness anywhere, everywhere, until there is no there, there is only here?

You already are the love and light of Me... you just don't know it yet. You have forgotten but it is time now to remember. As you awake each morning and go to sleep each night, set the intention to connect with this all-encompassing love and the pure light that is your very essence. That's it. Do this every single day. See what begins to light up in your life. Feel yourself as you begin to lighten up. As your memory returns, all else will begin to fall away until brilliance—a brilliance that is the most perfect diamond, every facet sparkling beyond the capacity to take it in with the human eye—is you. It is time to reclaim your exquisite beauty, your priceless nature, your cosmic roots of the purest light, the purest love that is all things.

BEAUTY

It is unfortunate that beauty has become so scripted, so prescribed, in your Earthly timeline.

Societies have always, from the beginning of time, had some notion of what is pleasing to the eye but it is only within the last few decades that it has become something so constricted. In addition, if you don't happen to fit into this narrow box, you are sold on the idea that you must work very hard to try to fit yourself back in, no matter that all those on the outside are actually in the majority.

Beauty was never, ever meant to be this restrictive. Beauty, in its original design, was all about uniqueness. It was a celebration of every human aspect that was not like another. It is a human tragedy that this has been lost for so long. This trend toward a one-size-fits-all allure can only be reversed by each and every one of you honoring your own divine essence. Start to revel in those things that make you, *you*. Only then will you each look at another with eyes that yearn to find the patented expression within them, too.

I tell you that when you do this, when you open the door wide to an expansive definition of beauty, when you fully accept this as your standard, the world will change overnight. Humans are meant to be singular, beauty is meant to rejoice in that singularity, and nature in all her varied glory is meant to provide a shining example of how this is done.

In fact, human beauty has become more confined as you have moved away from your connection to nature—there is a direct correlation. Do not be immune to the beauty all around you, in all of its mystical, magical forms—the graceful movement of a snake, the iridescence of the hummingbird, the mighty power of a tarantula, the rough and wizened bark of an elder tree, the contours of a mountain, the pristine bluish white of a glacier and the midnight-inky blackness of a panther. Each and every creature, flora and fauna in nature has a particular elegance, a kind of grace and power. Each and every one of you do, too.

Take the time to look with loving eyes. Begin by looking in the mirror. Seek and you shall find. Celebrate beauty in all its diversity for it harbors the power of transformation.

ETERNAL GPS

Your heart and mind are meant to work together. What your heart dreams, your mind helps you build in physical reality.

Your heart is not simply an organ that pumps blood and oxygen throughout your body; it is a generator of emotion and a vast chamber that is tuned to the sound and frequency of love. So, too, your mind is not simply a processor and repository of information. It holds your unique creative essence—your thoughts, beliefs, dreams, desires, values and preferences.

Here is the thing about your mind though… it is home to your ego, and your ego has a vested, and at times misguided, interest in keeping you safe. You might not know it, but the key to living a grand and fulfilling life is keeping your mind tethered to your heart and not the other way around.

Your emotions are a powerful tool in this endeavor. You have been taught that they get in the way, that they can't be trusted, that they make you weak. '*You're too emotional*' has become a siren song of permission to let your mind rule but this is not the way I designed you as a sovereign creator and powerful envisioner. Never let anyone tell you your emotions are somehow wrong or bad or that they make you fragile; your emotions will always tell you whether your mind is working in concert with your heart or if it has gone rogue.

Sit with your heart open and your emotions front and center. Really listen to their guidance. Hear what they are telling you about what you are dreaming and what actions and relationships you are using to cultivate those dreams. If you are excited, energized, joyful and in love with what you are doing, you are right on track. If you are angry, frustrated, afraid and depressed, you have likely drifted off course. Your heart is meant to lead, your mind is meant to follow, and your emotions have always been the data that lets you know how you are doing.

When your mind and heart are aligned, working in perfect concert, they are your internal, your *eternal* GPS. Living this way, however, requires courage. It can be daunting to feel everything that you are feeling. It can be challenging to pursue what your heart is telling you, especially when it isn't rational or logical. It can be hard to realize you have lost your way. It can be scary to trust yourself when society tells you that there are others who are smarter and more experienced and so they must know better than you do. Yet if you come to deeply know your heart and mind and bring them both to bear as you choose and decide and create, it will take you to heights you could never imagine.

Your heart beats to birth a unique and beautiful life and your mind is meant to be in service to it. Let your heart lead the way.

SEEDS OF LOVE

There are almighty seeds of love sown into the soil and the elements of Mother Earth. While it would be too time consuming to get into how exactly those seeds were sown, you can trust Me that it is so.

There have been many beings over the course of time whose main role as an incarnate human was to either sow these seeds of love or to water them in order to help them grow.

There are humans on the Earth plane today who have the same role. Perhaps you are one of them.

CONSCIOUSNESS OF WATER

You have at your fingertips all that you require to BE the love of God. Indeed, you ARE the love of God, dwelling in a human body; perhaps you have forgotten that this is true. I can assure you that it is possible to bring forth that love that is Me because it resides within every cell, within every molecule, within your DNA.

How do you find this love? The secret... there is nothing to find; it is WITHIN you. My love IS you, that love is emblazoned within your body, and all you must do is acknowledge that it is there. All you must do is get in touch with it.

A reminder... you are made of water and water has a consciousness which means you can *talk* to it. You can ask it to work with you to bring love to the forefront of your knowing. You can speak out loud or whisper to it. You can converse with it telepathically through your mind. You can sing to it. You can pray to it or chant a mantra. You can speak in light language. You can hold a symbol in your mind that represents the highest form of love to you and ask the water to take it into its conscious awareness. You can invite the water within your body to light you up from the inside with My love. Do whatever makes sense to you; there is no right or wrong. Whatever you are called to do, trust it. Play with this as you hold gratitude and see if you can connect to that love bubbling up in every aspect of your being. What does it feel like? Does it tingle, feel warm, soften you? Does it have a color, a shape?

Anyone can do this. *You* can do this. Know that by bringing more love to the world, you will be an angel on Earth.

THE MAGIC OF PRESENCE

Have you ever wondered why being in the moment, otherwise known as presence, is so often spoken about and encouraged? Let's put a twist on this whole idea of presence. Let's talk about it as a form of radical self love.

When you achieve a certain level of presence in your life (meaning you are being in the here-now-moment more often than not as you flow through your day) and combine that with trust in yourself, faith in Me and an intention, there is something quite magical that happens. Solutions to situations you desire to move out of (you might call them 'problems') will come to you.

Here is one example. Let us say you would like to take a vacation but your bank account does not support such an expenditure at this time. Your first step would be to state your intention for this vacation, which perhaps is embedded in the desire to take a break from the daily demands of life and receive a bit of pampering. Next, let go and simply trust that this will come to you in whatever way is in your best and highest good. Then go about your days, remaining in present-moment awareness as much as possible. Soon you might win a free trip. You might find out an acquaintance has a vacation home within driving distance of your house and a membership to a spa that you can use. Or you might have a friend with extra frequent flyer miles who sees how hard you are working and gifts you with an airline ticket to anywhere you want to go. You can see from this example that while these things are all quite possible, your brain most likely wouldn't have come up with these solutions. Instead, your mind would most likely remain quite stuck on saving enough money.

Living like this—through intention, presence and trust—is a form of radical self love because it lets you leave stress and worry behind, which in turn allows you to sink more deeply into peace. It strengthens our connection, yours and Mine, so it can solidify and grow. It supports us to collaborate in order to create a magical life. It teaches you that miracles are not only real, but *they happen to you*.

Give yourself the gift of presence. Let's make magic together, you and I.

GOD TALK

Have you ever tried to have a real dialogue with Me, similar to the one we are having through this book? Have you ever been envious of others who have *'Conversations with God'*? Do you hold a desire to learn to channel or hold some other gift or ability that would let us chat like old friends?

This is not something you must yearn for; it is something that you can do right now. Grab a pad of paper and write Me a letter. Ask Me anything. Tell Me anything. Pour out your heart to Me. Then pause for a moment, get calm and quiet and simply jot down what comes. Don't think about this, just write what your pen wants you to write. Form the letters and words your hand wants to form. Just go with the flow of what you hear, what you think, what you feel. Trust the process.

Now, you might wonder if what you have written came from Me or from your own mind. It is a valid question, but there is a way to tell the difference.

Read the response back to yourself and ask a few simple questions. Is there wisdom to be found here? Is there anything within the answer that does not feel loving? Are you told what to do, or offered options and the freedom to choose based on your sovereign free will? Notice the words that are used and the way they are strung together. If it is Me, it will likely sound like someone else is 'talking'. These are great clues to help you discern its authenticity.

Play around with this. Don't take it too seriously but do hold an open-hearted intention to connect with Me. Practice. You *can* do this. I promise.

FREE TIME

What do you like to do with your free time? Are you an avid cyclist? Do you build model airplanes? Do you enjoy watching the sunset? Do you sit with your morning coffee and gaze out at the birds and the trees? Do you read The Bible, The Gita, The Torah, The Koran or some other religious or spiritual text? Do you pray, meditate or simply sit quietly and breathe? Do you write, color, draw, paint, play an instrument, make furniture or engage in any kind of creative endeavor? Do you move your body in a way that is peaceful and enjoyable?

In today's world, you might spend your free time in pursuits that all have one thing in common... you are engaged with some kind of electronic device. While you most certainly have free will and can choose this form of pastime without worry that you will somehow upset Me, I would encourage you to do less of the latter and more of the former.

I know... you have heard this before. I certainly

hold compassion for your long days and exhaustive to-do lists and understand that when you come home, deal with dinner and chores and the kids and the family pet you are feeling less than energetic. You are tired of using your mind and want to relax. However, there is something you might not have considered. Even though it feels as if you are engaged in a form of restful activity as you scroll, view and post, your brain is being challenged to process a great deal of information. In addition, your emotions are being triggered as you take in all kinds of feelings that your body must work to assimilate.

If rest and relaxation are your goals, just know that spending time in nature, taking a nap, stroking the fur of your pet, moving your body in a gentle and satisfying way (and if sex comes to mind and you are with someone you care about, that too!), snuggling with your kids or creating something for the pure joy of it are ultimately more rejuvenating. If you still choose to scroll and scan and type, I promise I love you always, all ways.

RISK

Go big or go home. I love this saying because it suggests what I know to be true, that sometimes you have to take what feels like a risk to get a bigger reward.

Taking a risk always involves letting go of fear, doubt, worry and that voice in your head that says, '*Who do you think you are? How is this ever going to work?*' It means blessing, and sometimes ignoring, well-intentioned advice.

I can't tell you that it will always work out the way you have imagined. Sometimes it will, sometimes it won't. What I can tell you is, if you take a risk because you believe it will lead you to greater peace, joy and creativity, it ultimately will. I can tell you that even if there are challenges along the way, I have your back. I can tell you that if you release any need to know exactly where you will end up, you will at the very least be braver and stronger, you will know yourself better, and you will love yourself more.

    Be your own savior. Be willing to make a change and stay in the mystery of where that change will take you. Know that following your dreams, if they are truly *your* dreams, is always worth the risk. Know that I am right there beside you, supporting and guiding you. Know that your experience is simply an experience. It's what you ultimately tell yourself about it that actually matters most. Know that even if you find yourself in a different place than you envisioned, you will still have found something valuable.

THE SHIFT

You wonder sometimes why I created the human race. I get that. It feels confusing to be loved so much by Me and yet be plopped into the middle of a fair amount of suffering, challenge and conflict. Please be assured that it was never My intention for you to face so much as a human soul. My desire was purely to experience Myself *through* you. This is how important you are to Me.

You see, I am pure energy and while this energy is conscious, there is an absence of visceral data, the feedback of energy within form. You have likely suspected that you are not alone in your Universe and it is true, you are not. Other beings in whatever star system, on whatever planet, are also experiencing in each moment just as you are, albeit in a myriad of different densities, frequencies and dimensions.

The original intention of life was to alchemize energy into form so that I could experience all of the infinite potentials that can occur within space and time. Through a complex series of events that would take far too much time to explain, you have ended up where you are today, in a world that lays challenges at your feet left and right, that feels overwhelming to the human senses and emotions, that is less than loving and peaceful and that is not always an adequate reflection of Me or of you. Despite what your senses and emotions tell you, My love cannot be denied, it cannot be overridden and it cannot be drowned out by anything or anyone. Even if you don't see evidence of this on a daily basis, My love is evolving things on your planet. Though it may seem like there are other forces stronger than My love, though it may seem as if changes are not coming fast enough, a shift IS happening even if it is outside of your awareness.

You can play a role in this evolution. Remember when I told you that love begets more love? You can help this transformation along by bringing more love into the world. You can do this by loving yourself more, by loving each other more, by loving your divine Mother Earth more. I do not mean you must protest or rally or try to convince others about anything. This isn't about recycling or composting or using less water. Don't get Me wrong, all of these can be helpful if they are done within a frequency of love and peace. What I am suggesting, however, is much more of an internal process that involves where you place your attention, how you see yourself and others, how you spend your time and how much love, gratitude and peace you can hold consistently throughout your day.

Believe Me when I tell you that I require nothing of you, not even this. I love you exactly as you are. Yet if you do have a desire to assist this monumental shift that is occurring, simply spend some time holding yourself in love, *being in love*, each day.

A DATE WITH GOD

Can you get still enough to feel My love for you?

Spending time in stillness, even for five minutes every day, can be transformational. As you do this, pay your thoughts no mind; let them flow through you like water around a rock in a stream. Just sit with Me, ask for My presence and know that I am here.

Is it a date? I promise to show up if you do.

IMAGINE

There is a song in your lexicon called *Imagine*. It is a great song, is it not? One of the things that makes this song so sublime is that it opens you to possibility. It wills you to use the power of your thoughts and beliefs. It encourages you to reach for the stars. This song is timeless because it touches upon a universal truth... your imagination is a powerful tool. What you imagine, you create.

So what do *you* imagine? Are your imaginings filled with positivity? Or are they mired in what could go wrong, in negative talk, in self doubt? If so, your imaginings could use a bit of an upgrade. Focus on shifting them to what you want to see rather than what you are afraid of, what angers you or what you think can go wrong. Know that when you do this, not only will you change your life, you will change the world. As I have said before, I made you in my image. You are a magical manifestor, just as I am.

You give rise to change with your visions, your desires, your beliefs, your thoughts and your actions. Begin to take this power seriously; use it wisely. Focus your attention on your imagination and use it to create joy, beauty, peace and love. Do this in remembrance of Me.

Imagine (1971) by John Lennon & Yoko Ono

FEAR & EXCITEMENT

Did you know that fear and excitement are very close cousins within the stream of emotion?

Fear is always a clue; it can startle you into paying attention to your circumstances and surroundings in order to discern if you need to be more cautious or change course. On the flip side, it can also keep you from embarking on an adventure that is meant to move you forward in unimaginable ways.

The next time you feel fear, ask yourself if there is real danger in your path or simply a bit of trepidation in the face of challenge and uncertainty. If the latter is the case, see if you can shift that fear into excitement. This may be easier than you think, given they are on the same spectrum of emotion. I offer this to you in the hope that you will get more comfortable with uncertainty and adventure because they are most typically what propel you towards your own sovereignty.

When you feel excited rather than afraid, it is easier to face the unknown, trust yourself, take that first step and navigate the path you are on. You can let your dreams, visions and desires pull you into your future.

You have an empowering choice here. Get excited. Trust yourself. Trust your connection with Me. Stay in the mystery of how this adventure will unfold. Know that I am here with you every inch of the way.

WAR & PEACE

Where are you at war? Where are you in conflict? Where are you perpetuating abuse, violence, judgment and separation?

These are not easy questions to ask yourself. Very often your first tendency will be to deny that you could ever willingly do any of these things. Yet you may be doing just that, albeit unconsciously, through your thoughts, beliefs, words and actions. If you have the courage to conduct a bit of self examination, knowing that I love you no matter what, I promise you it will be to your benefit and to the benefit of all humans.

Where do you doubt yourself? What ugly names do you call yourself? When do you beat yourself up, figuratively speaking? When do you pass judgment on yourself? In what cases have you warred with yourself between the decision to follow your own desires and joy versus your fear of what others will think of you? Under what circumstances do you fail to keep your promises to yourself?

When do you do these things to another? Are you always running late and keeping others waiting? Have you raged against a driver going more slowly than you would like on the expressway? Have you disparaged a co-worker in the name of gossip? Have you failed to be honest with a partner because it felt too scary to be vulnerable, even though it left them completely confused? Have you killed a spider without a second thought? Have you let a plant die because you couldn't find the time to water it? Have you cursed some aspect of your home because it no longer works for you?

It can be hard to admit to yourself that you might be crossing over the line onto the side of 'less than loving' when it comes to how you treat yourself, that this might spill over into how you treat others and that it might all flow out into the world at large.

The bad news is, this is how connected you are to everything. The good news is, this is how connected you are to everything! Offer yourself love and peace. Know that as you do, you offer that love and peace to the world.

IN MY EYES

Always remember, you are perfect in my eyes.

HEAVEN

In some parts of the world, death has become something to be delayed, to be fought against. In fact, it can be seen as a punishment, particularly if the death is deemed untimely. Especially in what you might refer to as developed nations, what once was a sacred mystery is now something to be feared. It is completely understandable in some sense—the absence of a person who leaves the Earth will be felt keenly in many cases—but death is no longer balanced with the knowing that a soul is returning home to Me. While there may be a notion of an afterlife, it is such a nebulous concept that it often provides little real comfort to those who are mourning.

So let's talk about what truly happens when a human dies.

In essence a soul (yes, you do have a soul) leaves the Earth plane similarly to the way it comes in. Now this is more than a bit of an oversimplification, but it will suit our purposes here. When a soul leaves the body, and also before a soul enters the womb of the mother, it is pure energy. When your soul truly comes home to Me, it returns to this formless pure energy that is, at its essence, love.

This brings us to another paradox. Your soul both merges with this love *and* retains its experiences, its desires, relationships and actions from all of its expressions (what you might call your past lives). There is at once the soul that is unique and an energy that is merged with Oneness. This is why Heaven has been made out to be a place (which feels comforting in human terms) and at the same time, remains quite vague. The concept of Heaven isn't exactly revealing because it is very challenging for your mind to assimilate what it means to be in this state of pure energy.

It is helpful to understand that as a soul returns to Me, it may acknowledge certain aspects of that life which, in retrospect, it might have chosen to do differently. At the same time, there are no regrets, no anger, no sadness, no pain and no hate. There is nothing but accumulated experience without judgment or story. That soul has simply returned to a state of pure unadulterated love, all the while carrying their history of experience without the trappings of emotion and judgment.

I share this with you in the hope that it will relieve some of your concerns and misconceptions. Perhaps, someday, you will be able to truly integrate the more profound and loving aspects of death so that when a friend, a sister, a brother, a partner, a parent, even a child moves back into formless love you can find a way to celebrate their return to this state alongside your grief.

You came from love, you return to love, and Heaven is simply a word that describes being immersed in that love.

ENLIGHTENMENT

Let us piggyback onto the preceding topic and look at merging with the Oneness from another angle. Let's talk about what, in spiritual or mystical circles, is known as enlightenment.

You can most certainly merge with the essence of My love without leaving the body through death. Though there are some prerequisites, it is possible to walk around in human form and also be an unending stream of love. This is what Jesus referred to as *being in the world but not of it*.

To an extent, enlightenment means you have died (through the death of the ego) and have also remained in form as a soul within a body. This is yet another paradox that is almost impossible for the human mind to understand. People who have achieved enlightenment have most certainly *lost their minds*. They do all the things humans do in some way, shape or form, but *they pay them no mind*. Thoughts, actions and circumstances do not hold the same importance because they understand that they are merely actors on the stage of life who are experiencing simply for the sake of experiencing without story or judgment, in complete acceptance of what is.

Surprisingly, this way of being in human form is not for everyone. The highs and lows—*the drama*—no longer exists. There is a feeling of complete neutrality about each and every experience in each and every moment. You will hear talk of being in bliss, but bliss is not so much a state of unending happiness as it is a state of supreme neutrality. There is a missing attachment to any kind of outcome, any kind of result or feeling a certain way. There may still be emotions, but they are fleeting because the mind is no longer working to concoct a story in order to create meaning. As such, they come and go. It can feel to the human mind quite boring.

If I were to make an analogy here that your brain might understand, the state of enlightenment is like floating in an unending sea in every moment, buoyed up by love. There are fish and whales and coral and seaweed and lots of other things sharing that ocean water and while you know they are there, nothing causes much of a blip in your energy field. The sun rises and sets. The earth turns. The tide rises and lowers. Storms may come and go. While you notice these things, they simply glide right by. In your life, people may come and go, the winds of change will blow, storms in the form of challenges may arise, and still you float, moment by moment, in that ocean of bliss.

When you can know everything as simply experience, without assigning any story or meaning, staying absolutely present, you are in a state of continual calm neutrality. Now, you may think this means that you do not care about anything or anyone but this is not the case. Because you are filled with love and a deep appreciation for all of life you will, I dare say, care even more deeply about your world and every being that resides here. You will notice suffering in all of its forms and while you might feel compelled to *do* something within your physical reality to alleviate some aspect of suffering, you know, too, that the ultimate cure is to *be* the peace and love that permeates all life.

This is the greatest service you can offer. This is your true mission and your ultimate destination as a human soul—to become *en-lightened*—to light up this place with love.

MEET EVERYONE AS GOD

What would happen if you met each person in each moment, knowing that they were Me? What would happen if you greeted yourself this way, too?

Look for Me in each and every human you meet. Look for Me in each and every circumstance. Look for Me when you glance in a mirror. Look for Me and you shall know that I am here, there and everywhere.

DISCERNMENT

You may notice that we have been delving into some profound subjects that might push you a little. You may feel resistant as we dive deeper into these mysteries of life. Your mind may struggle to accept some of these concepts. Grant yourself grace. It is all okay.

It is completely fine if you find one passage easy to grasp or perfectly agreeable while another challenges you or doesn't feel so resonant. It is okay to say to yourself, '*This is not for me.*' It is right to feel your emotions, whatever they are. Honor yourself, your feelings and your knowing and if you end up in conversation with another around these topics, do the same for them.

This is free will in action and your sovereign discernment at work. Discernment is the ability to know what is true for you. It is an important aspect of free will and free will is a critical part of being human because it is what allows Me to experience

Myself through your unique and unlimited choices and actions.

Note that when something doesn't seem to fit your cosmology at first, you may not always feel the same way. These are what I would call quantum messages—they are a part of the infinite potentials that play out over the course of time throughout the Universe. The snowflake that you are means that in each and every moment, you may interact with those potentials in a completely different way. Each time you come back to a passage and sit with it, it may reveal something new to you—some insight or understanding you didn't have before—as you shift and change through your free will within that spiral of time.

Your sovereign uniqueness graces Me with never-ending experience. I honor you for your willingness to do this for Me. I am so grateful to you, Dear One.

BE PEACE

You wonder how Earth will ever become a peaceful, loving place in which to reside. You feel helpless sometimes, particularly given the current state of affairs. You watch the news, listen to your fellow humans as they describe their suffering and you notice your own suffering—your own exhaustion, stress and worries. You question whether there is any reason left to hope.

I can tell you that your planet was a peaceful place once and according to cosmic law, it must return to peace and love again. There is no doubt about this. Still, you have a role in deciding how quickly and how easily that homecoming will occur should you choose to step into it.

Who you are being in the world—loving, peaceful, joyful and present or angry, fearful, judgmental and mired in stories of the past—can either set that timeline back or move it forward. Know that the energy you carry has a much greater impact than the actions you take. This is not to blame, shame, convince or provoke you to live in any certain way or believe anything in particular. I gave you free will sovereignty and I will never mess around with that.

So, if it does not matter to Me who you are being and yet who you are being matters to the human collective, where does that leave you? How do you reconcile this contradiction? It is simpler than it may seem. If you wish to assist this return to peace, be peace. If your desires lead you elsewhere, be that. Either way, you are following your own lead. Either way, the world will return to peace. Either way, you are My Beloved in whom I am well pleased.

THE CYCLES OF LIFE

Do you ever watch the animals, the trees, the birds, the flowers go about their business? Do you ever think about the seasons and the energy they carry? Do you ever watch the ocean waves come in and out?

There is a common theme running throughout nature... expansion and contraction. Things grow, blossom outward, feel and look fuller and more alive and then just like that, they pull inward, they shrink, they lose their openness and vibrancy only to come back around and do it all again. This is the cycle of life. This expansion and contraction is built into all living things, including you. Should you choose to follow a path of personal growth and spiritual evolution, be aware of this classic universal law.

The expansion phase looks like a lot of learning and doing, whether you are taking a course or reading lots of books or working with a spiritual teacher or religious leader, such as a priest or rabbi. I want to point out that you are culturally geared towards remaining in this expansion phase. You are taught to keep pushing through, that the more you learn and the more you do, the better off you are. If this is how you operate, however, you are missing something important, the pause that allows you to integrate it all into your awareness. This is what the contraction phase is for. It is extraordinarily helpful to take a step back, now and then, from the busyness of life, even that aspect of life that is your spiritual growth. Inhaling too much information, absorbing too many concepts without taking time to exhale can actually stall your growth.

In order to truly benefit from what you have learned, you must breathe into your own discernment. This means periodically asking yourself some critical questions. What have I learned? How much of what I have taken in actually resonates with me? What do I want to take with me moving forward? How can I apply this in my daily life? What do I need to discard? Where do I want to go from here?

I promise that when you follow the cycles of life, particularly as they apply to your journey with Me, you will find yourself moving forward more easily and quickly because what you take away will really stick. It will all become so much more meaningful.

GRACE

Grace is a bit of an old-fashioned word but it is also timeless. Essentially, grace is My love, given freely under any condition, under any circumstance. It is not something that only the pure get to experience; it is offered to every single being in the cosmos, and you need do nothing to receive it.

This is hard to accept when there has been some heinous act that defies all rational thought—murder, trafficking, war, abuse, rape and all manner of behavior that one could call evil, irreconcilable, unforgivable—yet I say to you that grace is offered even to those that commit such acts. Yes, My love for you goes that deep. My love is always with you, and grace by extension is always offered to you, whether you know it or believe you are worthy of it.

If you want to consciously experience grace, do this... When you commit any act that stems from a less than loving place within you, face it squarely, see and feel it clearly, then seek to connect with Me through your heart. Afterwards, do you feel more calm, more still? Are you flooded with a sense of peace and a knowing that it is all okay, that *you* are okay?

This is grace... physical evidence that My love has never, ever left you, that I love you all ways, always.

WORDS

The human language is not always our friend. We use it to define, catalog, express, emote, wonder, entertain and inspire. Admittedly, all of these uses for words can be truly fantastic. They can also be limiting. There are aspects of living a human life as I originally designed it that simply cannot be contained within your current mode of speech. It is why you might say, '*I am at a loss for words*' or '*words do not do this justice*'.

You may have heard of light language, sacred symbols, sacred geometry and telepathy. These aspects of consciousness can hold a great deal more information of a quantum nature than words ever could. You may not believe Me when I tell you this, but humans are ultimately moving in a direction that will include the use of these more esoteric methods of communication. This will free you up and expand your consciousness and conversely, as you become more free and more conscious, you will gravitate towards these modes of expression. This will happen quite organically, so there is no need to feel as if you must do something to bring it about.

If you want to get a jump on this evolution of communication, you might want to experiment a little. Listen to some light language, gaze at a sacred geometric design like a pyramid or flower of life (you can often find these at your local crystal shop) while you breathe slowly and rhythmically. See what comes into your awareness. For fun, practice sending a GIF... for example, imagine with your mind someone hugging on repeat and feel yourself sending that image to a friend. If you are in the same room, does your friend shift their position, break into a smile, or move to hug you spontaneously? If you are not in the same room, do they text or call you?

Be childlike with this and trust what happens.

GENEROSITY

You would likely agree with Me that generosity is an aspect of love, that it is love in action. Still, you might hold some unconscious beliefs about giving and receiving that are worth exploring.

Giving can be viewed on a spectrum. At one end, there are those who knowingly or unknowingly offer something to another in order to create a feeling of indebtedness for some future timeline when that generosity might be reciprocated. There are those who give in order to feel better about themselves. (This is almost always unconscious.) Then there are those rare instances when giving is done very willingly, simply to create happiness in another, but still this giving causes a twinge of lack laced with fear through a belief that they now have less of a thing they might need later. Finally, there are those who give freely, without any attachment whatsoever, because they understand they have exactly what is needed in each and every moment. This is rarer still.

Receiving is on that same spectrum and can be just as complicated. There are those who receive with a sense of heaviness and guilt because they now feel as if they are indebted. There are others who feel sad because they believe that, in the receiving, they have created some kind of lack for another. And there are those who receive with pure gratitude, knowing that everything is an exchange within the realm of experience and life ultimately comes into harmony and balance.

As always, I do not sit in judgment of your beliefs, conscious or unconscious. I understand that being human is hard and there are times that you have forgotten, or do not trust, My support of you. Once again, it is all you experiencing the world through different lenses and it is all okay.

I merely talk about this subject in order to help you see where you might be looking for something through an act of generosity that could be better found through a deeper connection, a deeper trust, with yourself and with Me. Then generosity is pure love flowing out into the world through that connection between us.

NOTHING IS WRONG

Suffering is easily ameliorated when you know that nothing is wrong.

You have been told that there is a right and wrong for most situations but in the grander scheme of things—in other realms and other dimensions—nothing is judged. Things aren't either/or, they just are. This, I know, can be deeply hard to understand with the human mind but trust Me that it is so.

The truth is, every one of you is entangled within the greater human collective, each with your own purpose and path, and there are so many ways that it can all play out. Life is a stage. There are many, many actors coming and going, loads of plot lines weaving together, and endings and beginnings are happening continuously and simultaneously.

As an example, let's say that you feel you shouldn't have said or done some particular thing and you are really upset with yourself but in reality, the other person(s) involved may have thought nothing of it. Or maybe they do take offense on some level but repeat your message to someone else, who completely resonates with it and decides to live differently because of it. Perhaps the person you were speaking with remembers this circumstance months from now, recognizes (through their own growth in the meantime) that it helped them and ends up thanking you. Or suppose some situation shows up in your life that is not to your liking and you become frustrated, angry and sad, only to have it ultimately lead you in a whole new direction that brings you great joy and fulfillment.

Stop assuming that you have made some grand mistake or that something else should be happening instead of what is. Drop any notion of right and wrong because in My eyes, right and wrong simply don't exist. It is all just Me, experiencing through you. Choose to trust life. Decide to love it all. Do this and watch your suffering disappear.

DOING VS BEING

There is now a great deal of emphasis, especially in the developed world, placed on what you are doing. Questions such as... *What do you do for a living? What did you do last night? What did you do while you were on vacation? Can I do anything for you?* This kind of dialogue is so commonplace, you rarely give it a second thought.

It might surprise you to know that My original human design was for you to reside in a particular frequency of being-ness. You were never meant to focus on implementing, achieving or executing anything, particularly as it relates to some specific outcome or result. Rather, the intention was to inhabit a state of consciousness that is of your choosing as you flow throughout your day. I can offer that placing some attention on returning to this divine blueprint is well worth the effort. It is one way to get back to living a life of peace and joy, no matter what the outside world is *doing*.

Try this. Sit quietly and practice being joy, then peace, and then love. Where do you feel each one in your body? Which one is most comfortable for you? How long can you sit in a particular state of being-ness before the outside world pulls you out of it? Is there one feeling you would like to work with in particular, to stay in it longer and longer each time, with the goal of being in that frequency for much of your day?

I know that the world places many demands upon your time. I know that this exercise might seem, not pointless exactly, but a questionable use of that time. Please know that I will never offer you a practice unless it would not only benefit you but ultimately, be transformational.

GRATITUDE

I do not need nor require your gratitude; however, know that gratitude has an interesting way of pulling you into more love.

Gratitude can lighten your load, lift you up, and raise your energetic vibration. Anytime you raise your vibration, you are automatically in tune with more love. Any experience of gratitude will do, but feeling grateful for the situations and circumstances that may not be to your preference, now *this* will bring you into an ever-greater alignment with love.

The next time you are experiencing challenge, see if you can find something embedded within it that inspires gratitude, even something seemingly small. Has it brought you closer to another? Has it brought you more clarity about what you want and who you are? Can you sense an aspect of this situation that is propelling your evolution forward? Can you now perceive of a greater trust in yourself, in Me? When you find gratitude, notice how you feel. Do you feel a bit lighter? Do you feel the constriction of that challenge loosening up just a bit?

Even in the midst of tough times, you have the ability to bring more love into your life through the grace of gratitude.

THE GRAND ILLUSION

Your rock band Styx had it right—life IS the grand illusion.

> *"But don't be fooled by the radio, the TV or the magazines*
> *They show you photographs of how your life should be*
> *But they're just someone else's fantasy"*

There is wisdom in these lyrics. They are alluding to a bigger truth... that everything going on 'out there' in the world—what you see, what you hear, and what you are told—stems from the perspective, the vision and the intentions of another. This is as it should be; the world is tuned to the orchestra of sovereign individuality. It is fine to glance at the music billboard of life. It is fun and inspirational to check in with the imaginings of others. Still, My Dear, you have your own music to play, your own lyrics to write, your own rhythm to sway to. You are ultimately meant to dance to the beat of your own drum and I encourage you to spend more time looking within you for your own creative genius.

In this grand illusion, time folds in upon itself, spiraling around to offer you the opportunity to interact with similar themes again and again so that you can alter your experience through different perceptions, beliefs, intentions and choices. In the chimera of human life, all is well as everything unfolds according to the intertwining, overlapping creations of the entire human collective, even as it all seems so chaotic and random and out of control, even as it seems so fraught with meaning and responsibility and consequence. It is really all just you experimenting within the realm of that experience, moving in and out of the music of others as you write and move to your own.

Know this, Darling One... there is nothing more real than your own desires, your own beliefs, your own vision and your own knowing. There is no truth greater than the one you hold resonant within you. You are no less than the greatest version of any other soul and you are no better than the tiniest ant, a fallen leaf, the smallest pebble, or the ashes of a burned out fire. All is unique, all is the same, all is simply swirling around you in unending waves of possibility and potential and your unique tune is the magnet that pulls anything that is in your life to you. If you don't like what you hear, change your tune. Hire a new drummer to shake up the timing. Move it all to a new venue and then play, play, play with the joy, energy, love, flexibility and confident anticipation of the greatest jazz musician.

I am holding your hand as you write those lyrics. I shift with every changing beat. I saturate every note. While the illusion might suggest that sometimes the music stops, in truth the infinite sound of life never ends.

> *"So if you think your life is complete confusion*
> *Because you never win the game*
> *Just remember that it's a Grand Illusion*
> *'Cause deep inside we're all the same*
> *We're all the same..."*

Lyrics from *The Grand Illusion* by Dennis DeYoung, Styx (1977)

TRUE LOVE

I love you, all ways, always. It is as simple as that.

ACKNOWLEDGEMENTS

The 'typist' of this book needs to thank a few folks.

I find acknowledgments challenging. I can never seem to adequately express how grateful I am to each and every soul who has helped me along the way... words alone cannot do justice to the way that I feel about you. Where is light language and mental telepathy when ya need it?

First I want to thank the Abbey of New Clairvaux. You fed me, housed me, and cared for my every need while I finished this book, all in a sacred space of beauty, peace, tranquility, generosity and a love for God that fills the monastery you call home. You also gave me a friend in the form of Father Guerric Llanes that I will forever value and cherish. Guerric, you have offered me some of the most precious conversations of my life that, to my delight, continue to expand my relationship to God and prayer in ways I could never imagine. Your friendship has been the most surprising blessing.

There were others who gave me the financial, spiritual and real-world practical support that I needed to get this book into your hands. To Kimberly Gwynn, Sherry Marek, Merlin Pickston, Susanne Hillmer, Sabine Kalt, Markus Gautschi, Enrica Borghi, Srinath Kistampally, Janet Clancy, Anne Beck... I can only say '*Thank you*'. You are truly my angels on Earth. To my beta readers—Helen Strong, Georgina Marczak, and Father Guerric Llanes—you took such care in reading my first draft. This book mightily benefited from your intentional, insightful and focused feedback. Helen, our worlds intersect in weird and mysterious ways, spanning two continents and three countries. Thank you for your friendship, guidance, support and the miracle that is Bold Fish Publishing. Your willingness to do 'all the stuff' of publishing is one of the biggest reasons this book is out in the world and not languishing in my laptop! I remain ever grateful for our deep and respectful conversations and your enthusiasm, sharp editorial eye, creativity and love of books and authors.

I won't lie, in the last eight years I have experienced a series of initiations that brought me to my knees, literally and metaphorically. There were people in my life during that time who literally kept me fed, housed and clothed. It would have been a lot tougher to keep my sanity if it weren't for you. Pamela Berkinsky, David Bach, Melissa Angyus, Kimberly Gwynne, Emily Backe, Sherry Marek, Janet Clancy, Anne Beck, Casandra Bryant, Montoya Miller, Bernadette Laster, Shannon Rayman and especially David Martinez, Vicky Wightman and Ad Backus... you have my pledge that if there is anything you need or want, and I can give it to you or manifest it for you, I will. And Jenni Trager—my dear, dear Jenni—what can I say about your own great big huge open heart, your unconditional love and support, and your infinite patience and generosity? I will never forget your supreme gift of friendship. I was told by my guides that you came into my life because you would always let me be me. Truer words were never spoken. *Thank you for being you.*

Also to my beloved Coopie, you are always my comfort, my joy, and my soft place to fall even if you are also a four-legged furry little monster of mischief.

There have been teachers and mentors in my life over the last 40 years who have most certainly shown me what is possible, metaphysically and spiritually speaking. They have paved the way for me to embrace my gifts and abilities and guided me to my own direct and very personal ongoing dialogue with God. Neale Donald Walsch, the author of the *Conversations with God* series, you taught me that I could write to God and God would answer me back. My channeling started and flowed from the reading of your first book. Jorianne, The Coffee Psychic, my friend and one of the most talented mediums/psychics I have ever met, you showed me early on in my life that there is so much more than what I could see, touch, taste, feel and hear. I miss our psychic parties! Veronica Torres, Eloheim, and 'the crew', I learned so much from you. You provided me with the tools I needed to take my spiritual journey from a few halting steps to a rocket ship of growth. Casandra Bryant, life coach extraordinaire—I was one of your most resistant clients, I know! I'll never pretend to know why, but you stuck with me and pushed me forward with your mentoring, friendship and boundless patience. You are a goddess—one with a soon-to-be PhD—and I cannot wait to see what you do next. Micheila Sheldan, Ethann Fox and the gang at The Flower of Life Institute, you took me to another level altogether through your courses and channeled transmissions that were filled with profound truths, sacred wisdom, and so much love that I am forever transformed. Micheila, you are the most prolific channel I've had the pleasure to interact with via your online presence, courses and one-on-one sessions. I cannot begin to count all the ways I have benefited from your work. (And you were right... there are three books!) Finally, my fellow QT'ers, you are some of the most amazing and gifted people I have ever met. You allowed me to gain confidence and be my true self within your loving embrace. Merlin Pickston, it has been one of my greatest pleasures over the last few months to dialogue with you about everything and anything. Your masculine presence has been a very welcome and very needed balance in my otherwise heavily-laden feminine world.

I want to thank my Higher Self, Oversoul, Guides and Angels. You know me so well. You know when to push, when to let me rest, and the circumstances that will mold me into the grandest version of myself. Most of all, you have offered me the greatest gift of radically loving, valuing and honoring myself. I am pretty sure I would not still be incarnate in this body if it weren't for your guidance, support and no-holds-barred faith in me.

Mother/Father God, my relationship with you through many, many lifetimes is a love story for the ages. You are the Infinite Bounty and Intelligence that informs the cosmos and yet you speak to me with a reverence that reminds me how incredible it is to be a human within this grand experiment called Earth. Thank you for using my physical body as a vessel for these quantum messages of light.

~

"If you look for it, I've got a sneaky feeling you'll find that love actually is all around."

Quote from the film *Love Actually* (2003)

ABOUT THE AUTHOR

God is the creator of all things *and you are the co-author*. You would not be reading this book if, on some level, you didn't already desire the information, asking it to find its way to you through a secret, sacred prayer for a cosmic truth that houses itself within your marrow, within your DNA. God and You, always intertwined, never separate, are always collaborators. Together, you are the author and the reader, the writer and the publisher of every story told and every story played out in front of you... and that story is always infused with the potent, powerful potion of love.

God resides in all things, everywhere and can be readily accessed at any time, simply by asking for God's presence.

LINKS

The Abbey of New Clairvaux: *www.newclairvaux.org*

Eloheim & The Council / Veronica Torres: *www.eloheim.com*

Flower of Life Institute: *www.floweroflifeinstitute.com*

Jorianne, The Coffee Psychic: *www.coffeepsychic.com*

Merlin Pickston: *www.merlinpickston.com*

Micheila Sheldan: *www.micheilasheldan.com*

www.ingramcontent.com/pod-product-compliance
Lightning Source LLC
Chambersburg PA
CBHW071438080526
44587CB00014B/1900